A PHILOSOPHY OF IDEALS

BY

EDGAR SHEFFIELD BRIGHTMAN

BORDEN PARKER BOWNE PROFESSOR OF PHILOSOPHY
IN BOSTON UNIVERSITY

NEW YORK

HENRY HOLT AND COMPANY

To

MY STUDENTS

PREFACE

This book is intended to sketch the outlines of a way of looking at ideals which seems to me to be true, but which in neither the only possible nor the most popular way at present.

If we wish to reach rock-bottom in our thought about ideals, we must consider both their function in the organization of experience and also their place in the universe beyond man. One may hold the view that experience and nature are brute facts, having nothing ideal in them, yet capable of being more or less subdued by man and so used for ideal purposes. This is what seems to be the testimony of ordinary experience and is the essence of many current realistic and pragmatic philosophies, represented by such distinguished men as Bertrand Russell, George Santayana, and John Dewey. On the other hand, one may hold that experience and nature are, in some sense (as philosophers delight to say), actually ideal systems, deriving their meaning and even their very existence from their embodiment of ideals. This view — more daring, more speculative, but, I believe, more fundamental than the other — is defended in this book. It is the view commonly called idealism. The two views agree on the utility of ideals in human experience. But the one view holds that ideals are no more than human utilities — inventions for maintaining human existence in a cosmos indifferent to ideals. The other view finds in them a revelation of the very structure of the real world beyond man.

This little book is presented to the public with no vain hope that it will settle the high dispute. But perhaps it will call attention to some aspects of the problem of ideals which are overlooked by many writers or disposed of in too facile a way.

The first three chapters, in another form, were delivered as the John M. Flowers Lectures at Duke University in November 1927, and Chapter IV as Phi Beta Kappa Address at Allegheny College in June 1927. I gladly express my thanks to *The Journal of Philosophy* and to *The Personalist* for allowing me to use as the basis of Chapters VI and VII articles which had appeared in those journals under the titles of " Modern Idealism " and " Tasks Confronting a Personalistic Philosophy."

E. S. B.

Newton Center, Massachusetts
April 7, 1928

CONTENTS

A PHILOSOPHY OF IDEALS

CHAPTER I

MIND

Every honest person is an idealist in the sense of being devoted to some ideals, if only to the ideal of honesty. But there are great differences both in the ideals to which men are devoted and also in their interpretation of the function and importance of ideals. All agree that some ideals are false, and that some are mere social conventions of only passing utility. All agree that other ideals are truer and higher. But there is disagreement about the nature of the true ideals.

Classical philosophy has usually regarded true ideals as revealing something about the objective structure or meaning of the universe. Recent realism, pragmatism, and humanism are also earnestly devoted to ideals, but they usually regard them as functional devices for adjusting the human organism to an unideal world. They adopt the " hypothesis of the indifference of nature," as Guyau puts it.[1]

According to the classical view, ideals are man's discovery of and adaptation to the ideal structure and promise of reality itself. According to the other view, ideals are simply tools for the mastery of a nature which cares nothing about them.

Two different conceptions of the aim and value of human life here stand opposed to each other. It is not honest to smile amiably and remark that all philosophers really mean the same thing in different words. Two radically different types of civilization are striving for the mastery. In the worlds of business, of labor, of literature, of religion, of politics, and of law the conflict is felt. There is much of the smugness of victory on both sides; but from no point of view, intellectual or practical, is the smugness justified. Neither of the positions, as commonly held, may be wholly true; both cannot be.

If we are to think fruitfully about this or any other problem, we must begin where we are. If we begin where we are not, we must tell how we got there, which is sometimes embarrassing. "Where we are" is our own mind. All that we perceive or dream, know or guess, hope for or hate, must first somehow be an object of our own mental experience before we can talk about it. It must justify itself to the mind if it is to be acknowledged as true. The problem of mind is central to the problem of ideals and indeed to every other problem; for all problems and all solutions are at least works of mind, whatever else they may also be.

Mind, our starting point, is very hard to describe or define. As soon as you talk about it, you interpret; and interpretations differ. Mind, I believe, is not body nor any movements of body; yet when I say this I part at once from all Watsonian behaviorists and materialists. But if mind is not body, you cannot point to it as you point to a physical object or process. Yet you can indicate what mind is. Mind is consciousness. All experience, from the rawest sensation to the most intellectual reasoning, is the realm of mind. This includes all our consciousness of physical things. The things themselves are not in my mind, but all of my perceptual and other consciousness of them is in my mind.[2] The whole mind, then, is all consciousness which belongs to what I call " me "; all my experience. The word " self " is a synonym.

It is convenient, however, to distinguish between " self " and " person," letting " self " mean any consciousness no matter how elementary, and restricting " person " to those selves which are capable of reasoning, value experience, ideals, and reflective self-consciousness. All animals are selves; perhaps plants are; perhaps even electrons are elementary selves. But probably persons are confined to the higher forms of life.

I

If we wish to understand the mind, we naturally turn to the science of the mind, psychology, for enlightenment. But the light that is in it is darkness. Much good work on details has been done by psychology; but when it comes to telling what the mind as a whole is and what its higher processes are, psychology is in a state of confusion. The *Psychologies of 1925,*[3] a report of a series of lectures delivered at Clark University, lets some of the various schools come to expression through their spokesmen. The result is chaos.   No wonder that Jared Sparks Moore had inquired into " The Foundations of Psychology." [4]   No wonder that Hans Driesch writes of " The Crisis in Psychology." [5]   Knight Dunlap, it is true, finds that " psychology to-day is in a highly satisfactory condition," but he reaches this conclusion by regarding behaviorism as dead, psychoanalysis as a bog and a " horrible example," and the unconscious as a self-contradiction. [6]   The peace in his psychology is very decidedly with victory — for his point of view.

The schools of psychology are as numerous and conflicting as the schools of philosophy and for much the same reasons.   Structuralists hold that mind is to be understood in terms of its constituent simple elements; functionalists find understanding not in elements but in process and adjustment.   Freudians would explain the conscious in terms of the unconscious; some physiological psychologists would explain it as caused by the nervous system.   Extreme behaviorists would deny or ignore consciousness entirely and would study only the reactions of the physiological organism.   Persons rejoicing in the designation of epiphenomenalists would admit that there is consciousness, but would hold that it causes nothing and is of no explanatory value. [7]   These persons seem to lack the courage either to be thorough behaviorists or, on the other hand, to treat mind seriously.   Germans have developed a new point of view, called the *Gestalt*-psychology, which holds that experience does not consist of simple elements, as structuralists believe, but of configurations called *Gestalten*, which can only be understood as wholes. Still other psychologists see in purpose or striving for an end the basic nature of mind and the key to its explanation, as opposed to the mechanism of many other theories. Others, again, emphasize the fact that all consciousness belongs to some self, and that this is the most important feature of mind. The last three types have much in common. But it cannot be said that there is any agreement on what mind really is or how its unity is to be understood. Psychology is at the present time one of the most important, probably the most popular, but, barring sociology, the worst of the sciences.

The inquiring mind will seek for the root of this evil. Can it be that all of the schools, except the one which you and I profess, are led by blind guides? (This seems to be Knight Dunlap's point of view.) Can it be that everyone is wrong except thee and me? — and (you will recall) sometimes I think that thee is. This cannot be, unless we are to give up all faith in human intelligence. It is more probable that every standpoint affords a more or less partial and incomplete view of mind, which would be supplemented and corrected by a fuller view. But even this explanation fails to account for the confusion. Men have been studying the mind for centuries — ever since Aristotle's *De Anima*.[8] Why has it been so much harder to grasp the meaning of mind than to understand matter? Why has psychology been so much slower than physics? It is the fashion to say that theology, with its interest in the soul, has had a deleterious effect on psychology. Perhaps. But the grip of theology on physics has been loosened; and it is hard to attribute the divergences between John B. Watson and Sigmund Freud to the malign influence of the Pope. Again, perhaps philosophical speculation — or the lack of it — has interfered with psychological progress. But philosophy has usually encouraged the scientific study of phenomena. It is not clear that philosophy has affected psychology more than it has affected physics.

What then is the source of the difficulty? It seems to me that the trouble with psychology lies primarily in no external influence upon it, but rather in the very nature of scientific method, or at least of preconceptions about scientific method, as applied to the peculiar subject-matter of the mind. Scientific method begins with observation and leads to explanation. Now the observation and the explanation of mind are peculiarly difficult.

If we consider observation, we note that the other sciences, certainly all natural and non-psychological sciences, acquire their data by sense-perception. That is what observation means for them. But the immediate data of psychology, although *given* in present experience, must be *observed* by introspection, that is, by looking into the mind. Hence the psychological observer is restricted to his own mind. No amount of present experience or of introspection will give him an immediate view of another mind. Sense-perception of the behavior of the bodies of other people gives you necessary and valuable clews to their minds; but the clew is not mind itself. It distresses

the scientific conscience of many a psychologist to have
to build his science on first-hand data which are strictly
confined to his own mind. But this distress is imposed
by the nature of experience and psychologists should en-
dure it manfully instead of seeking to escape from it by
the expedient of trying to find mind as something that
can be perceived by the senses.

Hence experimental observations of strictly mental
facts are very difficult. We can observe and control
stimulus and response; but the psychological fact is
neither stimulus nor response nor their combination in the
reflex arc, but it is rather what happens in consciousness
during the whole process. Consciousness of the stimulus
is not the same fact as the stimulus; and consciousness
of the response is not the same fact as the response.
Rational thought is more than delayed response. Experiment, it is true, has direct access only to behavior,
except in the case of the so-called " subject," whose verbal
reports of his experiences are accepted. But the subject's words as they reach the experimenter's ear and mind
are not the same fact as the subject's actual consciousness. Thus consciousness seems to elude experiment, except in so far as the experimenter engages solely in intro-
spective observation of his own mind.

Moreover a psychological experiment finds itself caught
in a peculiar circle. The experimenter wishes to study
mind; but in order to study mind he must be a mind.
That is, he has to presuppose his subject-matter and, so
to speak, bring it with him. He cannot observe it exter-

nally and wholly objectively, as the physicist thinks he observes material objects. It is awkward for an investigator to have to presuppose what he is investigating. But the awkwardness is imposed by reality itself and the investigator will remember Bacon's words, *natura vincitur pariendo,* "nature is conquered by obeying her."

Not only is observation subject to unusual difficulties in psychology, but also explanation is of a different sort in at least three respects. In the first place, most of the natural sciences (except biology) seek mechanistic or deterministic explanations. The interest has been in finding the causes which necessitate the observed effects. In psychology, too, mechanistic explanation has shown itself useful. But the experiences of purpose and freedom are obstinate and do not lend themselves readily, if at all, to mechanistic treatment. The fact that mechanism has succeeded in other sciences has given many psychologists a mechanistic bias. They have looked for the machine-like aspects and the machine-basis of mind, and that is what they have found. You find what you look for. But if you look at the mind as a whole, you find its behavior different from that of a machine, and you need a different principle of explanation — the principle of purpose — in order to make its behavior intelligible.[9]

In the second place, the other sciences have flourished by the method of analyzing the given into simple elements. But a mind is a peculiar sort of reality which is not made up of simple elements. You cannot add sensations and hopes and fears together to make a mind. These experiences exist only as functions of a whole mind. Hence, mind (as purposive, *Gestalt-*, and self-psychology agree) cannot be fully understood by analytic method. It needs also to be studied as a whole, functionally and synoptically. This differentiates psychological explanation from the predominantly analytic method of mechanistic sciences. All science tries to find some constant, something continuous, the laws of which constitute the science. For the physico-chemical sciences continuity is found in simple elements, atoms, or electrons, the combinations of which follow definite laws. But there are no analogous continuous elements in mind. A sensation, unlike what we naturally think an electron to be, ceases when we are not conscious of it. The continuity of mind is found in its identity as a whole self, rather than in the constancy of its elements. This is a hard saying for those who wish to model psychology on traditional physics; but it arises from the very nature of experience.

In the third place, the other sciences have usually succeeded in reducing qualitative differences to quantitative ones. But psychology has almost no quantitative laws to its credit, except where the relations of physical stimuli or conditions to mind are being measured, or statistical methods are used. Mind consists largely of the experience of qualities, and quantitative explanation abstracts from quality. The quantitative physics of red color is not concerned with the qualitative psychology of redness. For a long time, perhaps permanently, psychological explanation will have to take the form of a description of qualities rather than a measurement of quantities. This offends against prejudices based on scientific method in other fields, but follows from the very nature of mental experience.

All of the difficulties in observing and explaining mind combine to drive home the truth that both the laws and the methods of a science should be derived from the subject-matter studied, and not from preconceptions, even those acquired through the study of other sciences. Mind is mind; and the student of mind should take mind as he finds it. If so taking it he has to depart from the methods of other sciences, he need not be disturbed. If his investigation should have to be so many-sided and unique that his study turned out to be very unlike other sciences, he may as well face the facts. It may be that a science of mind, in the strict sense, is impossible because science is always abstract, while mind is the most concrete of objects. It is concrete not as being visible to the senses, but as being a rich system of connected experience. Hence W. E. Hocking remarks that " a kind of metaphysical psychology is the only satisfactory science of the mind." [10] Philosophy, and not science, aims to apprehend the full concrete meaning of life.

We have been trying to find the sources of the current confusion in the study of mind. It appears that the difficulty arises especially from the differences between mind and physical objects, combined with the fact that psychologists often seek to study mind by methods suited only to physical objects.

II

One of the chief differences between mind and physical objects as they are ordinarily understood is its immediacy. When we speak of the immediacy of mind, we mean the fact that it is actually present. We do not have to guess or hope or infer that we are conscious, or that our experience exists. Consciousness is given as an unescapable fact. But the objects of physics and chemistry do not appear to be immediate or given in the same sense as mind is immediate and given. Certain perceptions occur in my mind; I interpret them and infer the existence of molecules and electrons. But even if an electron could be suspended directly before my eyes, all that is meant by the electron could never be actually a part of my mind. Observation and knowledge are acts of mind; but the thing observed or known may be an entity which never has been and never will be a part of my mind.

We may even go further and say that not only is mind immediate, but also nothing but mind is immediate. All that ever can be immediately present is mind. Science and philosophy seek to discover the cause or stimulus or interpretation of what is present in the mind. But all of thought and life is only an elaboration or explanation of what is at some time given as present experience. You look through a telescope. All that you actually see and think and feel at the time is your own conscious experience, but you observe, then calculate, and infer that there is an object other than your present experience called the sun and situated some 92,000,000 miles away. But your experience of the sun is literally your experience — one of the many experiences which as a whole constitute your mind.

Datum

There has been a great deal of discussion in recent philosophy centering about the problem, " What is the datum? "   The word datum means " what is given." The view which I have just presented is obviously the same as saying that the mind (or the self) is the datum.[11] But it would be most misleading were I to give you the impression that the plain and simple tale of mind that I have been telling would be believed by all. In fact, there is very wide divergence of opinion about the apparently elementary question of what the present experiences are with which we all start and which are immediately certain.

It may serve to clarify the situation if some of the other views are stated and considered in relation to the proposition that the mind is the datum. Some philosophers, especially certain English realists, believe that the datum is simply a sensible appearance, such as all the sense qualities which we find, colors, sounds, odors, shapes, and the like. This theory carefully avoids using the ordinary term " sensations," for that would mean that the data are in the mind, and the thinkers who accept this theory of sense-data desire to avoid any reference to the possibility that these data may be in mind or consciousness.[12] But if the sense qualities are not in the mind, I find it difficult to see how they can properly be said to be given. After all, as G. Dawes Hicks points out, " experience does

not begin with separate sense-data." [13]   The starting-
point, rather, is the whole complex of experience, including rational, affective, and volitional processes, as well as
sensory qualities.   The so-called " sense-datum " is like
a " pure sensation " which William James rightly held to
be " an abstraction." [14] We never meet a sensation of
color all alone; we always meet it in company, that is, in
a mind.   And a sense-datum of a sort which is not even in
a mind is doubly abstract.   There may perhaps be, some-
where in the universe, a redness which is a mere sense
quality and nothing else; but our knowledge that there is
such an entity depends on a long series of reasoning and
such redness is thus not a datum but an inference from
data.

The critical realists have a somewhat similar view.
For them the datum is what they call an essence. By an
essence is meant simply a quality of any sort. [15]   It is certainly true that we experience qualities. But essence and
quality, like sense-data, are logical abstractions and not
the actual concrete starting-point of experience.

Others, especially some pragmatists, think that the
datum is the biological situation. We start as organisms
in an environment to which we respond and adjust. This
view is true of our biological history. But it is not true
of our psychological history. The very knowledge that
we have a body and that there is an environment is the
outcome of thought about our experiences. Biology is a
scientific achievement; it is a system and not a datum
either for an infant or for a biologist. The notion that

we start with the biological situation is a sophisticated
outcome of scientific reflection, not an account of the experienced datum with which we are presented at the start.
Bodies and real objects, as the critical realists rightly
hold, are not given, but may be known or inferred from
the datum (whatever this mysterious datum is).

Where, then, are we? Are mind and hence nature and
ideals all lost in hopeless confusion? The reply is that
they will be unless we can think our way out of the morass
in which our present philosophy is sinking. As we look
about for help, a contribution by J. Loewenberg of the
University of California proves enlightening. In an article in the *Journal of Philosophy*,[16] he distinguishes between " pre-analytical " and " post-analytical " data. Applying his distinction to our problems, it is evident that
the notion of the mind as datum means experience as we
live it and find it *before* the work of analysis; while abstractions like " sense-datum," " essence," or " biological
situation " are arrived at after analysis, and so are post-
analytical. Loewenberg shows that much of the confusion is due to using the same word, datum, to mean both
what thought must start with and what it must stop with.
This helps us to center on the question about the pre-
analytical datum, which is, of course, the beginning of all
knowledge and experience. Regarding that datum,
Loewenberg makes a fruitful suggestion. He says that
it is not a thing or a quality; it is merely a problem｜ This
suggestion seems to be more fundamental than many
others that have been offered. To use an illustration that

is not Loewenberg's, let us suppose that my datum contains what I call " a ringing." When I first hear it, I do not know whether its cause is " in " a bell, " in " my ears, or merely " in " my imagination. But the ringing itself is certainly my experience; and my experience is a problem to me. In fact, one of the most certain truths about immediate experience is that we do not know what it means until after investigation, if then. The datum is, indeed, a problem. It contains conflicts and obstructions; it is incomplete and confused. But, if we accept as true all that Loewenberg says, a further question arises, namely, how can there be a problem except in a mind? A mere physical or metaphysical confusion is no problem until the confusion is present in conscious experience and a mind defines its problem. If, then, the datum is a problem as Loewenberg believes, it must be a problem in a mind. Thus we find ourselves compelled to return to the idea that the mind is the datum.

There is, it is true, a sense in which the datum is not a problem. About what is actually present to us there is absolute certainty and no error is possible. It is what it seems. If you are color-blind and see gray where others see red or green, there is no doubt that you do see gray, and no error about the datum. The datum is what it seems; it *is* seeming. But as soon as a question is raised about what the datum means, so soon error may arise. If the color-blind person asserts that when he sees gray there is the same physical stimulus present as when a normal person sees gray, he has fallen into error. His datum, consciousness of gray, is undeniably present, but his interpretation of it is in error. This truth was stated by Aristotle. " Each single sense," he said, " judges of its proper objects and is not deceived as to the fact that there is a colour or a sound; though as to what or where the coloured object is or what or where the object is which produces the sound, mistake is possible. " [17] Hence, out of the very certainty of the datum a problem arises.

The most certain fact, and the only absolutely certain empirical fact, then, is my own self-experience. To say that the mind is datum emphasizes at least four aspects of experience: (1) that we find relatively confused and " raw " sensations in experience prior to their elaboration by scientific thought; (2) that we possess an unanalyzed consciousness prior to the work of analysis and the reference of thought to objects and causes; (3) that our present conscious experience is the ultimate basis of all our knowledge of and belief in whatever is not now present conscious experience, or in other words, present self is the sole basis of confidence in absent objects; and (4) self-experience is a name for a trait of all consciousness and is to be distinguished from reflective self-consciousness, a relatively infrequent process in which we think about ourselves. The datum is always self-experience; but only rarely does it contain reflective self-consciousness.[18] We exist even when we do not think about our existence. This self-experience is an indivisible whole, yet ever-changing; private, yet in communication with other selves; present, yet remembering a past and anticipating a future.

The mind, then, is both datum and problem to itself. All perception, all reasoning, believing, doubting, hoping, and desiring are the mind's effort to answer the question, " What do I mean? " Every answer of science or religion, poetry or philosophy, must be tested by its relevance and adequacy to the datum-mind. What do I mean by my sensations, my moral nature, my aspirations, my pleasures — by my whole life? The problem of philosophy and the problem of life reduce alike to this one, " What do I mean? "

III

The datum-mind is certain; " je pense, donc je suis." But its present consciousness is not the whole story of a mind. Every mind contains principles which drive it beyond its present self. Time is one such principle, through which one part of mind sinks into the past, and a new part grows into the future. Desire and purpose are other such principles, which impel the mind to explore itself and its world. Logical reasoning also is implied by the nature of every present moment of mind; and reason drives mind from the mere datum to the conception of a whole mind and a whole world. But there is another principle which involves time, purpose, and reason, yet adds an important new function, namely, the memory. If memory were utterly to fail, I should be reduced to a mere datum which would be constantly changing, yet having no unity and no sense. The passage of time would be a meaningless flux; purpose and desire would be forgotten if their object were

attained; reason could hold no subject-matter before its
gaze. Without memory, the mind disintegrates and ceases
to be a mind. When memory functions it is a bridge
which leads from the present datum to the whole mind.
It is, of course, true that no memory can hold the entire
past of mind within its grasp. But many linkages of
memory from the present datum connect it with past data,
which, in turn, were connected with previous data.[19] My
whole self, then, includes my past, which means all of the
experience which is connected by such a series of linkages
of real or possible memory with the present datum. It
also includes that future which purpose and desire in part
anticipate and control and into which I am always growing by the inevitable passing of time. All this experience,
with its laws and capacities, is my whole mind. Well did
Martin Luther say that " life is no mere essence, it is a
growth." [20]

The present moment of any mind seems to be a poverty-
stricken experience. In itself it holds but little of value
or meaning. Yet memory, reason, and purpose unite it
to past and future perspectives which, as we rightly say,
give life a meaning, and make it worth living. May we
not say that the datum-mind of the present is significant
precisely in so far as it is effectively related to the whole-
mind? A good magazine is on a higher level than a good
newspaper; and a good book is on a still higher level.
Why? Because the transition from newspaper to book
is a transition from miscellaneous data to the systematic
unity of one mind at work. A mere momentary datum is

almost incomprehensible; it acquires meaning when related to the mind as a whole. Thus, every item in our daily papers would be meaningless to a visitor from another civilization, until his mind could grasp our history and our customs.

This view of mind as a whole has two important implications. The first has to do with the unity of mind; the second, with the nature of knowledge.

First, then, on our view, the unity of mind is a unity in and of conscious experience. I am one and the same mind, because I can remember enough to justify my confidence in the unity of my past with my present. This unity, resting on memory, implies the very important trait of time-transcendence. The datum which is my actual self of the present contains within itself events that have a beginning, a middle, and an ending by the clock, yet are grasped in one time-transcending act of mind. It is only because of this time-transcendence that I can think at all. In order to say " x is the unknown quantity," I must be able to hold in mind in one act of apprehension every idea from " x " through " quantity," and throughout this act remain one and the same mind. If " x " were in one mind and " unknown quantity " in another, algebra would never get a start. The unity and the uniting memory of the mind are possible because the mind grasps its experiences of time in an act that, so to speak, rises above time and looks down on it. Time-transcending unity does not, however, mean a mysterious abstraction out of all relation to time; it means only the concrete fact that mind can

grasp the passage of time without itself passing as fast
as the time does.

A second important implication of this view of mind is
the fact of self-transcendence. By self-transcendence is
meant the fact that the mind necessarily explains itself
as present datum by referring beyond that mere datum-
self to something which "transcends" it. I cannot know
my "whole self" without this category of self-transcendence; much less can I know other objects or selves without the certainty that in the present self there is the possibility of valid knowledge of what is not the present self.[21]
Thus present consciousness implies that other consciousness has been and will be actual, and that there is a world
in relation to which I stand.

IV

The mind, then, is a growing whole, living in an environment revealed by mind's self-transcending knowledge.
Studies of the environment and of mind's responses to environment constitute the various sciences. No one doubts
that there is an environment and that mind is unintelligible apart from its relations to the environment. But there
are tendencies either to identify mind with some aspect of
its environment (such as the behavior of the body) or to
overlook the range of the environment. It will, then,
serve to clarify our understanding of mind if we show
what view of the environment is implied by our view of
mind.

It may be remarked that any and every possible view of
the environment depends, at least in part, on one's view

of mind. But it is no more than just to say that the view of present mind as datum and of the whole mind as including past, future, and possible data, connected with the present datum by memory-, purpose-, and reason-linkages seems to make the environment more remote and problematic. Special stress, then, must be laid on the self-transcendence of mind and also on the fact that reason not only serves to unify the self but also to interpret its environing world. Without these qualifications the view of mind as datum might seem subject to the difficulties of the monads of Leibniz which have no windows. But self-transcendence and reason are windows through which the monad sees its environment. If there are still difficulties in the view, they are no refutation of it, provided it be, as it seems to be, a true statement of the facts. Who ever guaranteed that facts should be free from difficulty?

What then do the mental data imply about the environment of mind? As mind understands itself, it speedily finds reasons to justify the hypothesis that there is an environment. The belief that there is no environment — called by the traditional name of solipsism — asserts that there is nothing except present experience. But if this assertion means anything, it is an appeal to reason, and reason requires an explanation of the present data in terms of their relations to something else. That " something else " is partly the mind's own past, but chiefly the environment of mind. Yet the very belief that there is an environment, let it be repeated, is an hypothesis rather than an experience. It is a rational hypothesis. If you say, " There is no outer world — there is nothing but my own experience of here and now," you fly in the face of reason and refuse to think. Even your words "here and now" mean nothing except in contrast to an environing there and then. None the less, when you say, " I see a table and the table is there," strictly the first proposition, " I see a table," represents your datum, the experience in your mind, while the second, " the table is there," is a rational hypothesis which can never be verified except on the further hypothesis that the interpretation of the contents of your mind will shed light on what is not contents of your mind. What science calls a completely verified hypothesis must, therefore, rest on the deeper hypothesis that rational thought about experience can grasp reality, or, as Hegel says, that the actual is the rational (although Hegel does not regard it as hypothesis). Knowledge is possible, then, only because faith is reasonable.[22] We know that there is an environment because otherwise mind becomes meaningless.

But I do not see any way of compelling a wilfully un-reasonable mind (and there are such) to be reasonable or to accept reasonable hypotheses. D. H. Parker has put the case well: " He who refuses to make any sort of hypothesis, whose intellectual conscience forbids him to believe aught except the given, can never understand." [23] If, however, a mind acknowledges that it ought to be constructively reasonable, then its choice of further beliefs is in every case subject to logical criticism and is in no case merely arbitrary; for as soon as a mind becomes arbitrary it has abandoned its faith in reason.

Granting, then, that mind must acknowledge that it has an environment, of what does that environment consist? A complete answer to this question would involve a complete science and philosophy. We must be satisfied with a brief survey. The environment of any mind may be said to contain the following factors: (1) the biological, (2) the physical, (3) the social, (4) the subconscious, (5) the logical and ideal, and (6) the metaphysical.

The physiological organism, especially the brain and central nervous system, seems to be the nearest environment of mind. That brain and nervous system are environment and not mind itself is evident from the fact that most of the time the mind is not even conscious of having a brain and nervous system; that they are actual environment is shown by physiological psychology. Secondly, the biological organism is surrounded by a world of physical objects which stimulate it, and which become known to mind only as the organism is affected by them and mind draws inferences from the data arising from such stimulation. Thirdly, there is the social environment. Other minds, as individuals or groups, communicate with ours chiefly by means of behavior which affects our organism through physical media. But minds acquire the ability to understand other minds more and more intelligently and sympathetically as they interpret their attitudes, purposes, and beliefs. Unless telepathy be true, we cannot dispense entirely with physical symbols in communication with other minds; but as understanding develops, symbols are more and more heavily freighted with meaning conferred on them by minds. As symbol diminishes, meaning may increase.

Fourthly, it was said, there is the subconscious environment of the self. "What!" say you, "You have told us that my brain and my body are no part of me; now you say that my subconscious does not belong to me, but to my environment. You have gone too far." In reply I can only invite you to consider the facts. Is the subconscious ever present in the datum-mind? No, its very nature is that it is not a part of my conscious experience. Its *effects* are present in my consciousness, and my consciousness influences it; but if mind is wholly conscious experience connected by linkages of memory, purpose, and reason, the subconscious falls without the domain of my self-experience. Doubtless every subconscious process is itself a datum to itself, so that we may properly speak of every subconscious process as belonging to *a* self. But that self is not *the* self of my normal consciousness. It is true that there are borderland cases such as the fringes of attention and dreams; but these are not strictly subconscious; they belong, however vaguely, to the conscious self which is I. My subconscious has a unique causal access to myself, but its very nature precludes it from being part of myself. It is environment.

A very different type of environment is the logical and ideal. As we explore our minds, we discover that thought obligates us to acknowledge universal principles. Now a universal principle is a logical and ideal truth; it is not a particular fact to which you can point. Hence a logical concept or "universal" can never be identical with any single conscious experience of our mind. Our mind can "grasp," that is, can mean to refer to, universal truths; but in so doing it is referring to something more than its own conscious experience of the moment. What the "something more" in a universal really is, we need not now consider save to point out that in some way the realm of logical truth is an environment which my mind has to acknowledge.

Last of all, we spoke of a metaphysical environment. The experience of the race from time immemorial has included data which men have referred neither to their brains nor to physical objects nor to fellow men nor to the subconscious nor to logical abstractions but have referred directly to the being that makes all of these possible, the supreme reality, which religion calls God. Knowledge of God as environment of mind has to be based on faith, it is true; but so, we have seen, does knowledge of tables and chairs; and in all cases the faith must be rational. The relation of the metaphysical environment to the other types of environment may be very close, but that problem does not concern us just now.

The life of mind has been described in this chapter as a datum. While that word expresses the immediacy of mind, and was chosen for that purpose, it fails to express the ongoing process, the activity, and the freedom of mind.[24] These are most important and have been assumed throughout our discussion. These traits are especially evident when one considers the relation between

mind and its environment. That relation may well be
described in terms of stimulus and response, or adjustment, provided these terms are not defined in a narrowly
biological sense.[25]   The emphasis on these concepts by
pragmatists, notably by John Dewey, has chiefly been intended as a protest against a static view or any view
which cuts mind off from the processes going on in the
environment. The effect of this emphasis has been liberating and even inspiring. Mind has been seen to be an
active life, potent in a changing world. But this advance
has, for various reasons, been accompanied by considerable confusion and overemphasis on purely biological
situations.

It may be possible to hold the gains made by pragmatism and to add new territory, if we reinterpret stimulus
and response and adjustment in terms of the view of
mind as datum. For this view the stimulus is any power
which affects minds. It may perhaps originate biologi-
cally, or subconsciously, or logically, or in the will of God;
but wherever it originates it is a mental stimulus only
when it affects a mind. An event (if there be such) which
makes no difference to consciousness would not be a mental stimulus, no matter how it might cause a biological
organism to respond. And when a mind receives a stimulus, it receives it actively; that is, it responds. The character of the response will vary with the attention which
the mind gives to the stimulus, and with the extent to
which it draws on its whole resource of memory, purpose,
and reason, as well as on other factors.

Further, on our view the concept of adjustment acquires new meaning. Functional psychology has usually dwelt on the functions of consciousness in adjusting the biological organism to the physical (and social) environment. This point of view is entirely adequate for a purely biological interest. But G. A. Coe made a sound contribution to the understanding of mind when he distinguished between biological function and preferential function, and pointed out that " to be conscious " is " the first preferential function. " [26] Following Coe's hint, then, we may define adjustment not primarily in terms of a relation of bodily organism to physical world, but primarily in terms of the relations of mind within itself. After all, what does bodily adjustment amount to in the life of mind save as a stimulus or inhibition to mental process? If I were never conscious of my body and its adjustments, and consciousness went on regardless of body, I should not care whether body were well or ill, alive or dead. The adjustments that make a difference are the adjustments that occur within my actual conscious experience, hindering or helping its plans, paining or pleasing it, baffling or inspiring it. The study of the mind is then a study of stimulus and response and of adjustment; but the response and the adjustment must occur or be expected to occur within conscious experience before they have significance for a mind. The response to stimuli must lead to an adjustment of mind within itself before any environmental changes can be fruitful or significant to mind. Hence the life of mind is not so truly described in terms

of adjustment of organism to environment as in terms of adjustment of environment to mind. When the environment is itself mental, as in social and religious relations, the adjustment is mental, and some form of communication or coöperation occurs.— Consciousness, then, does not exist for the sake of biological adjustment, but biological adjustment exists for the sake of consciousness.

V

How, then, must mind be understood? We have found that mind is datum, mind is a whole system, mind is process, mind is self-identifying, time-transcending, self-transcending activity. It must therefore be understood first from within, as one's own conscious datum. Then it must be understood in the light of a full analysis of the datum. Then it must be grasped as a whole, as a true system. W. E. Hocking has well described this double process of understanding. " If you stand," he says, " on the plain and look toward a range of mountains one contour stands sharply separate from the contour behind it, the mountains are named from below. Look down on the range from the air, and you recognize the binding masses at their bases. It is the concrete which contains all the abstractions together with their relating roots." [27] Again, mind must be understood as active and purposive response to stimuli and so as self-adjustment. And finally, most difficult yet most essential, mind must be understood in relation to its environing world.

We found at the outset that psychology is in a grievous state of confusion, and we ascribed this confusion to the uniqueness of the mental subject-matter and to misconceptions arising from the nature of scientific method. In the light of our further study, we are now able to assign an additional reason for the difficulty. The complexity of the mind and of its relations is such as to require many different kinds of study. Persons interested in one special branch of psychological investigation find that branch so interesting that they easily develop a feeling that their approach is the only possible one. The true view of mind will be the one which includes the truth of all approaches to mind. It will not seek to annihilate structuralism or behaviorism, Freudianism or purposive psychology, but will venture to include the truth of them all in a systematic view which really explains and does not merely add together unrelated fragments. The outlines of certain aspects of such a systematic view of mind I have sketched in this chapter, assuming that all real *views* of mind are true, but that all are not on the same level of importance.

We have now considered the mind and its relation to environment. The next chapter, then, will investigate our view of nature, the physical environment of man. Then we shall be ready in the third chapter to think about the status of ideals, the problem with which we started. The first chapter deals with the self; the second with the world; the third with what they ought to be. Or let us say that the first deals with the subject; the second with the object; and the third with their perfection. We shall then be ready to consider the problems of ideals and idealism from other points of view.

CHAPTER II

NATURE

In the previous chapter a view of mind was set forth which is not now commonly held. It is, however, related to theories of the self such as have been developed by Descartes, Berkeley, Leibniz, Kant, Hegel, Royce, Calkins, Bowne, and other idealists of past and present. No one of these thinkers can be held responsible for the theory of mind as datum; but they all agree that the mind is immediately present to itself.

Now, there are numerous recent critics, often influenced by philosophical realism or pragmatism, who are very suspicious of views that regard the mind as any more immediate, present, or certain than the world around us. Such critics point to many considerations which show, in my judgment, that they have not clearly understood the idealistic view of mind. How, they ask, can mind be more present than nature, when nature so clearly determines the experiences and the very origin of mind? Such queries have no bearing whatever on the idealistic view either of mind or of nature, for to say that mind is the only datum does not in the least mean that mind by some magic causes its own existence or is the only existing reality. To say that mind is the datum leaves open the question as to

what causes mind. To say that mind is the most certain
reality does not end investigation, but spurs it on; for a
solitary present mind is a chaos until its relations to past
and present environment, as well as to its own past and its
own capacities, are understood.

The view of mind as datum merely prohibits the self
from being anything except itself. My experience of the
starry heavens above as well as of the moral law within
is my experience and belongs to my mind. The starry
heavens cannot be literally " in " my mind. Only I myself, in all my complex experience, can be there. But if
the fact that the mind is itself and nothing else were to
prevent the mind from knowing anything else than itself,
we should then be shut up within ourselves, and our philosophy would be " solipsism," the theory that I myself
alone exist. We have, however, found that the very nature of the self is to transcend itself in the act of knowing. " Transcend," like transcendentalism, is a lofty
word which may elevate the soul without enlightening
the mind. When I say that " the self transcends itself in
the act of knowing," I mean that my present consciousness may describe or refer to something which is not my
present consciousness. This is, indeed, always happening. When I say, " I see a man," I usually mean not
alone that I have a perceptual experience but also that
there is a man who is other than my perception. Thus in
everyday perception the self transcends itself, that is, it
describes something not itself. If that description is true,
we rightly say that " the self knows the man." All

knowledge rests on the fundamental hypothesis that knowledge is possible, and that a present self can know what is not that present self. This hypothesis alone can transform the chaos of present experience to a cosmos of orderly meaning, and hence it alone is rational. But it is an hypothesis, for, as Durant Drake says, "all realism . . . requires faith."[1] The hypothesis that knowledge is not possible flies in the face of reason. Unfaith is unreason. We can, therefore, answer the question, "What do I mean?" only as we answered it in Chapter I; "I mean that I am more than the present datum, and I mean that I in my whole history am related to a complex environing world."

But this does not satisfy a certain type of realist. He does not see how a mind can get outside itself to know something else. Even so profound and impartial a thinker as A. N. Whitehead says explicitly that if "subjects with private worlds of experience . . . be granted [and this protasis is our idealistic view of self] there is no escape from solipsism."[2] To this it may be replied that if knowledge is not possible there is no escape from solipsism, either. A difficulty which troubles critics like Whitehead lies in the meaning of "private." They seem to take it as meaning "shut off in every way from the rest of the world." But, in being the datum, the self is not shut off from knowing or interacting with the rest of the world, even though it does not literally contain any of that world or exchange any parts with it. The datum is private only in the sense that it *is* itself and nothing else.

My mind can never be nor contain anything except itself; yet it certainly can know and be known by, affect and be affected by, what is not itself. I am always in contact with my environment without ceasing to be myself. It would therefore appear that an idealistic view of mind can maintain itself against this realistic criticism.

But at one point realists have the advantage over idealists. In general, whatever idealists may say about the place of mind in nature, they have been more interested in mind than in the relations of mind to nature, whereas realists have been more objectively interested in nature. This fact has brought them the advantage of a closer relation to the natural sciences. Idealists, on the other hand, have sometimes seemed indifferent to the scientific explanation of nature. This fact has serious consequences for the idealistic view of mind.

Man's mind does not exist in a vacuum, but man is, as Pringle-Pattison puts it, " organic to the world." [3] It is true that I must experience myself only; it is equally true that I must infer a world if I respect reason. That there is communication between my mind and other-than-my-mind is just as certain, although not just as immediate, as the fact that my mind exists at all. Both nature and mind, then, need to be conceived in such a way as to make this communication intelligible. To try to make it intelligible in the extreme behavioristic manner by denying the conscious mind is logically in much the same position as the solipsistic method of denying nature. Both nature and mind must be affirmed and so defined as to make each other intelligible. Nature must be such as to explain our conscious experiences, and we must be such as to know and to deal with nature.

Some persons — and they are very numerous — will always be impatient with the philosophic quest for the solution of such problems. Mind and nature stand in actual relations, they say; what difference can our theorizing make? On the attitude of such people John Locke's remark is good comment. He says, " Though the familiar use of things about us take off our wonder, yet it cures not our ignorance." [4] A normal human being cannot prefer ignorance. Moreover, in the present case, as was shown in Chapter I, the whole question of the status of ideals in the universe is at stake, and no man for whom morality or art or religion or truth is of importance can fail to be concerned about such an investigation. We undertake, therefore, to face the problem, What do I mean when I perceive and describe nature? And, inseparably connected with it, the other problem, What is the place of mind in nature?

I

Nature is an infinite problem, but the objective problem of nature is rendered much more difficult by the way the word nature is used. It has had many different meanings and often is employed in a eulogistic or honorific sense, which surrounds the word with an emotional halo.

Mankind inevitably expresses its cherished beliefs in what may be called eulogistic words. It would be unrea-

sonable to veto all such words or the emotions which they
arouse; but it cannot be denied that the presence of the
emotional factor often makes clear thinking very difficult. At different stages in the history of thought different words have held the honorific position. For some,
the eulogistic word has been " Substance," for others,
" the Absolute," for yet others, " Evolution," or " Society." But the two supreme words have been " God "
and " Nature," appearing in some form in every philosophy and every religion, whether as the Brahma and
Māyā [5] of Hinduism or as the *" deus sive natura "* of
Spinoza, or as the Jahveh and his creation of Hebrew
thought, or the noumena and phenomena of Kant. Just
now we are to center our attention not on God but on
nature. From the early Greeks who wrote περὶ φύσεως
down to John Dewey's *Experience and Nature* and the
books by C. D. Broad and Durant Drake on *(The) Mind
and its Place in Nature*, nature has been a major theme
of philosophy. But this does not tell us what nature is!

We may approach an understanding of what nature
is if we consider what it is not. Nature is sometimes
contrasted with art, sometimes with the unnatural, and
sometimes with the supernatural. When contrasted with
art, nature means the state of affairs in the world around
us as it is apart from changes wrought by man. In the
broadest sense, art means human skill in adapting nature
to desired ends; in a narrower sense, it means either the
imitation of nature or the creation of a realm which shall
be more beautiful than nature. Nature as contrasted

with the unnatural means either the usual, the instinctive, or that which is adapted to the preservation of life. Thus the birth of children, thumb sucking, and eating are natural; while a miracle, or complete lack of interest in the opposite sex during adolescence, or suicide would be unnatural. Nature as contrasted with the supernatural means the world as we observe it through our senses, and the laws of that world. The supernatural means whatever cannot be inferred from sense-data or explained in terms of the physical order. Thus, the supernatural is the invisible and spiritual, the divine, as well as the miraculous.

But each of these conceptions of nature is obscure and ambiguous. Can nature be contrasted with art? When we consider the extent of the changes made by man in attempting to control and beautify nature, it may be questioned whether any of the air or water or soil of the earth remains wholly unaffected by art. Has art swallowed up nature? Where can the line be drawn? Or, if we seek to distinguish nature from the unnatural, we find that a nature from which everything "unnatural" has been subtracted is a greatly reduced, incoherent, and unsystematic nature — a nature that never really existed and could not be understood if it did. Every so-called unnatural event is as much a part of the system of nature as the most normal and inoffensive happening. This distinction, then, sheds no light. More may be said for the distinction between nature and the supernatural. But here also, questions arise. In the first place, many doubt

whether there is any supernatural. Then, granted that
there is a supernatural order, the problem of its relation
to the natural becomes acute. It may be questioned
whether mind is natural or supernatural. Such a distinction, then, must come, if at all, at the end and not at
the beginning of an investigation.

Instead of seeking to contrast nature with a not-nature
of some sort, we may regard nature as all that there is.
Indeed, the attempted distinctions between nature and
art and between nature and the unnatural suggested that
nature, art, and the unnatural all belong to one common
world, and are but differentiations within one system of
nature. If, then, nature be regarded as all that there is,
such difficulties as were found in contrasting it with something else are avoided, but at the cost of the loss of any
meaning — save the eulogistic — in the word. To say
that nature is all that there is, is not to say anything about
the structure or laws of nature. All-that-there-is is an
inclusive problem, a scrap-basket for all difficulties. Yet
when the word nature is thus applied to all-that-is, it is
usually not with the sincere intention of using it as symbol for a problem; rather it is a label intended to commit
one in advance to some special theory of nature, such as
"naturalism." Such a use is peculiarly confusing where
the problem of ideals is concerned. To say that ideals
have a purely natural origin and function may mean that
they occur within all-that-there-is and must be reckoned
with in our account of that " all "; or it may mean to imply that the function of ideals is solely to adjust a human

organism to its physical and physiological environment. We seem then to be pretty thoroughly confused about what we mean by nature.

There seems to be more clarity if, instead of either contrasting nature with art, the unnatural, and the supernatural, or regarding it as all-of-reality, we consider nature as the object of the sciences. We speak of natural science. But here also there is confusion. Etymologically the word " nature " is derived from the Latin *nasci* (to be born) and the word thus in its first intention refers to living organisms. Hence, many distinguish the natural sciences (*i.e.,* the biological) from the physical (*i.e.,* the physico-chemical). But this is doubly misleading. " Natural," as we have seen, comes from the Latin word meaning to be born, and "physical" comes from the Greek word of the same meaning. Not only are " natural " and "physical " etymological twins, but also the sharp separation between the "physical " and " natural " sciences is an act of violence in view of the fact that biological processes are capable of being described as chemical reactions.

But if we take nature to mean the object of the physico-chemical and biological sciences, the question arises whether psychology, history, sociology, and the like, are natural sciences. This question is no mere quibble about terms; it is of moment both to our thought about the unity of nature and also to the questions at stake between materialism and idealism. If you say that psychology is a natural science you seem to commit yourself to materialism; if you say that it is not, you seem to shut mind off into a realm apart from nature and turn it into something supernatural. Yet, if our study of mind in the previous chapter is at all sound, there really is a fundamental difference between our experience of mind and our experience of physical things, for the former is immediate, while the latter is always mediate and inferential. To be sure that I am conscious requires no reasoning of any kind, and not even introspection. Mere awareness of present experience tells me with absolute certainty that the experience is there. But in order to know with anything like equal assurance that my present experience actually confronts a real physical thing, I must carry on some experiments and I must think about them. Since, then, the roots of my knowledge of physical things (including living things, even my own body) are on a different level from the roots of my knowledge of myself, we can understand why the Germans distinguish *Naturwissenschaften* and *Geisteswissenschaften*, sciences of nature and sciences of mind. But both the differences within and the unity of nature are perhaps better recognized if we speak of physical nature and psychological (or psychical) nature. The former term would then refer to the objects of the physico-chemical sciences and the latter to the objects of the psychological sciences. In Chapter I, we have discussed psychical nature; in this chapter our chief interest is in physical nature.

The relation between physical nature and psychical nature is the theme of the greatest philosophies, appearing, as we have said, in the materialism-idealism controversy, and in all aspects of the mind-body problem. The greatest minds have found it difficult to be clear at this point. Kirchmann justly criticizes Aristotle for not making a sharp distinction between soul and body.[6] It is interesting to observe the persistence of this confusion in modern thought. Watson's behaviorism is a perfect instance of it. Similarly, a recent critic writing in the *Encyclopædia Britannica* says of Ernst Mach that " his whole theory appears to be vitiated by the confusion of physics and psychology." [7]   A. N. Whitehead remarks that " the effect of physiology was to put the mind back into nature "; [8] but his statement is to be interpreted in the light of his novel and difficult theory of what nature is, a theory which attempts, as does all sound philosophy, somehow to transcend the differences between the physical and the psychical and thus to work toward a unified view of the world.

If, then, we confront the task both of differentiating and also of relating physical and psychical nature, and meanwhile bear in mind our aim of investigating the status of ideals in the world, our problem falls into two parts: first, What is this nature which is the object of the sciences? and secondly, Is nature, the object of the sciences, all that there is?

II

Mind, the object of the psychical sciences, we have already described and we have seen that it is surely not all that there is. Its inner life is unintelligible unless we suppose an environment in which it lives and with which it interacts. There remains, then, the object of the physical sciences. Our present concern is to inquire precisely what that object is.

It is a strange comment on the perversity of human nature — even the human nature of learned and distinguished scientists — that some competent scholars have objected to the very raising of such questions as we propose. P. W. Bridgman of Harvard has recently undertaken a careful study of similar problems in *The Logic of Modern Physics*. " The world of experiment," he says frankly, " is not understandable without some examination of the purpose of physics and of the nature of its fundamental concepts." But, he continues, " until recently all such attempts have been regarded with a certain suspicion or even sometimes contempt." [9] He braved this irrational hostility, and we may follow his example, although approaching the problems in an entirely different way.

It may be said that there are two chief views about the object of the physical sciences, namely, the positivistic and the metaphysical. The positivistic view, briefly stated, is that these sciences are concerned wholly with the facts of experience, but not with their source in the nature of reality nor with the ultimate origin of experience itself. The metaphysical view is that the sciences reveal to us the true nature of reality as it is independent of experience. Any treatment of these views will have to be a sort of composite picture of the theories of many different thinkers and, therefore, will not represent precisely what is held by any one man. But this need not trouble us. We are concerned with truth, not with personalities.

The positivistic view, then, asserts that science describes experience and nothing else. It is empirical. Since experienced facts are " appearances " or "phenomena," it may be called phenomenalism. But there is great danger of confusion unless we bear two distinctions in mind. The first is the distinction between scientific and philosophical positivism. Philosophical positivism asserts that the experienced facts are all that can be known and that metaphysical knowledge is unattainable. Scientific positivism asserts merely that experience is all that science knows, thus leaving open the question of the possibility of metaphysics. We are concerned solely with the latter type. A second important distinction is that between sensationalistic and critical positivism. Sensationalistic positivism holds that the sciences are concerned only with objects which are actually given to the senses. Critical positivism holds that the sciences are concerned with the laws or ideal limits which are implied by and which explain sense objects.

Berkeley's " *esse* is *percipi* " and Mill's famous definition of matter as a permanent possibility of sensation are sensationalistic positivism. Such positivism is pretty thoroughly discredited to-day. Max Planck, the physicist, says that " the physical definitions of sound, color, and temperature are to-day in no way associated with the immediate perceptions of the respective senses." [10] Like-wise Ernst Cassirer, the philosopher, remarks that "any attempt to interpret the concepts of natural science as mere aggregates of facts of perception must necessarily fail. No scientific theory is directly related to those facts, but is related to the ideal limits, which we substitute for them intellectually." [11] But Cassirer accepts what we have called critical positivism when he says that the true hypothesis "does not go beyond the realm of the factual, in order to reach a transcendent beyond, but it points the way by which we advance from the sensuous manifold of sensations to the intellectual manifold of measure and number." [12]

Critical positivism, then, holds that science is not confined to statements of what actual experience has been or now is. For it, science consists of general laws about what type of experience may be expected under defined conditions. Hence it deals not alone with the laws of all actual experience, but also with the laws of all possible experience. And, since in its analysis of experience it arrives at descriptions of atoms and electrons and of the interior of the earth and of the sun, "possible experience" must be taken to mean not actually possible, but ideally possible. That is, an electron for science is the fact that if our senses or our instruments were sufficiently discriminating, our perceptions of the electron under those ideal conditions would conform to the laws of electronic physics. Thus the sciences are concerned with what is visible to the naked eye only as a starting-point; their real object is the laws of all possible experience — microscopic and ultramicroscopic, telescopic and ultratelescopic.

If Berkeley was a sensationalistic positivist, Kant was a critical one. Comte's philosophical positivism was based on the thesis that the positivistic character of scientific knowledge makes all metaphysics impossible. But Schopenhauer, Lotze, Bowne, Royce, and many others, have shared Kant's critical scientific positivism, while holding as against Comte that metaphysics is possible. Many men of science have held a positivistic view of their task.

Critical positivism leaves metaphysics an open question. Science, on this view, describes the laws of experience. But it gives us no knowledge about what ideals ought to guide us or what values we should attain. Science cannot either prove or disprove the truth of an ideal. Only a comprehensive view of reality, such as metaphysics seeks, can rationally justify or refute ideals.

It is true that antimetaphysical positivists like Comte, and many modern humanists, are passionately devoted to ideals; but neither their ideals nor (much less) their passion can be derived from or justified by a purely descriptive positivistic science. A paper like that of Victor E. Levine on " Spiritual Values in Science "[13] is therefore confusing. He says that " the chief usefulness of science lies not in the material advantages it offers the human race, but in the spiritual enrichment with which it endows the individual pursuer in particular and mankind at large

when it makes righteous employment of its applications."
This is quite true, provided no one supposes that the
spiritual enrichment from righteous employment comes
from science alone.   No natural science, physical or psychological, tells us that we ought to be righteous or what
righteousness is.   That we derive from our philosophy of
life.   Science alone does not dictate philosophical conclusions, if critical positivism be correct.   The scientist must
look to philosophical investigation if he is to define or
defend any ideals of the righteous employment of science.

The positivistic view of physical science has interesting
relations to the view of mind as datum.   If mind is the
only immediate datum and if science deals only with immediate data, the realm of physical things is simply a part
of the realm of mind.   This sounds like solipsistic non-
sense, but the "sound" is misunderstanding.   Sensationalistic positivism, if taken as a complete account of nature, is indeed solipsism.   But critical positivism does
not identify nature with the particular facts of my experience.   For it, nature is the whole system of the laws of
the actual and ideally possible experiences of all human
minds.   Furthermore — and this is even more important
— positivistic science does not pretend to reveal the inner
nature of reality or the power which produces it.   On
this view, then, physical nature is, as G. A. Wilson holds,
the resultant ideal construction in conscious experience
when mind is stimulated in a certain way by the creative
powers of the universe.[14]

This positivistic view is self-consistent and thoroughly

intelligible. But it is not accepted by all. Many hold to a metaphysical view of science, which asserts that scientific investigation leads to definite knowledge of the structure of reality as it is, independent of all our experience. All that can be known about the world is known by science. Science describes what was before any human experience began, what is whether human experience now observes it or not, and what will be after all human experience ends. The positivist would account for all of these realms by the concept of the laws of " ideally possible experience "; but the metaphysical scientist regards them as real in themselves and independent of all conscious experience. If science reduces matter to electrons and protons, then the holder of this view says that matter really is electrons and protons. If science shows that mind is wholly dependent on the body, then mind too must be wholly explained in terms of electrons and protons. In short, the metaphysical view of science, held consistently, is either philosophical materialism or naturalism, or else a dualism of physical and psychological nature. It arises, in the last analysis, from the belief that physics is metaphysics. L. T. Troland states this position when he says that " the physical scientist wishes to know the universe in its entirety." [15] Yet the physicist thus defined must be somewhat embarrassed by learning later in the same book that no part of consciousness is any part of the physical world.[16] E. A. Burtt states the metaphysical view when he says that " mind's gradually acquired knowledge of its surrounding world is wholly a discovery, not in any sense an imposition." [17]

But the metaphysical view, although widely held and quite in accord with common sense, is not without its difficulties. For one thing, the view is very hard to state clearly, as we shall see a little later when we come to compare the positivistic and the metaphysical conceptions. Again, if physics is metaphysics what shall be said of mind? If the physical and psychical sciences are equally true as descriptions of the real world as it is in its inner nature, we get a dualism like that of Descartes, who (as Whitehead puts it) held to " a materialistic, mechanistic nature, surveyed by cogitating minds." [18] This is a division of the world into matter which has no properties akin to mind and minds which have no properties akin to matter, two worlds which therefore cannot interact, yet miraculously do interact through the pineal gland, and are just as miraculously related to the one substance, God. This makes too many miracles. Descartes's dualism is not held in the strict Cartesian form by any philosopher to-day; yet something like it, or as improbable, is necessary if physical and psychic sciences are both metaphysical truth.

Another attempt to retain the metaphysical truth of the sciences was embodied in the hypothesis of psycho-physical parallelism. Starting from the Cartesian principle of the absolute difference between matter and mind, Spinoza abolished the subterfuge of the pineal gland and held that physical events have only physical effects and psychic events only psychic effects, but that no physical event has any psychic effects or *vice versa*. This view, developed in various forms by many thinkers, makes matter as impotent to affect mind as mind is to affect matter, yet it has the merit of being true both to the conservation of matter and energy and also to the fact that mind is datum, which we have explained in Chapter I. But it holds that for every event in each realm there is a corresponding event in the other; and the relation between these unrelated Siamese Twins is as puzzling as Descartes's interaction between relative substances which cannot interact. It is true that Spinoza sought to unite thought and extension in God as his attributes, but a relation between unrelatables is just as impossible in God as anywhere else, the more so if God be conceived as a reasonable being. Hence parallelism has been stated in other forms by recent writers. The double aspect theory, for instance, asserts that every electron or proton of matter has both physical and psychical properties, and that the mind and the brain are therefore different aspects of the same complex fact. But here the puzzle of Spinoza's God reappears indefinitely in each electron, and there are also substantially the same objections to this that may be urged against materialistic atomism, for a mystic psychic appendage to each atom complicates matters without explaining anything.

A panpsychism, like that of C. A. Strong, even when more clearly expounded by Durant Drake, helps very little, if at all. It holds that the stuff of which all matter consists is psychic, and hence that consciousness is the very substance of the cerebral process. To quote Drake's words,[19] the world is "psychic stuff arranged in a physical pattern," which means that mind is spatial. It also means that the stuff of an electron although " psychic " is not aware of anything; it lacks thought, sensation, emotion, and will. Such a view gives a certain unity to nature and saves the causal efficacy of mind which parallelism endangered. But after all the unity which is gained is purely verbal. If you regard electrons as metaphysically spatial, and as lacking awareness or any conscious trait, what good does it do to baptize them with the blessed name "psychic " ? The word is meaningless in such a context and a meaningless assertion is no assertion at all.

Thus the metaphysical view of science oscillates between what is essentially a materialistic denial of the experienced nature of mind as datum (*vide* Watson) and some sort of bifurcation of nature into matter which is always matter and a mind which is always mind — " and never the twain shall meet! " Such philosophy says to mind as Keats to the lover on the Grecian urn,

> Never, never canst thou kiss,
> Though winning near the goal . . .

Here, then, is our perplexity. If we take the positivistic view of nature, we have limpid simplicity but seem to be in danger of solipsism. If we take the metaphysical view, we find utter confusion in attempting to relate physical and psychic entities, but at least we are objective. Which of the two possibilities is to be chosen? It appears evident that we must choose between them.

If we find it hard to choose, we may be consoled by the

reflection that many others are in the same predicament. If you read John Dewey's *Reconstruction in Philosophy,* you are reasonably certain that his view of science is positivistic; but if you consult his *Experience and Nature,* you are equally certain that it is metaphysical. On the other hand, P. W. Bridgman starts out in *The Logic of Modern Physics* by accepting the " common sense judgment that there is a world external to us," and by limiting the inquiry of physics to " the behavior and interpretation of this ' external ' world " [20] — plainly the metaphysical view — and speaks of quanta, stresses, and other objects of physical investigation, as " forever beyond the reach of direct experience " [21] — thus appearing to exclude the positivistic view. Yet, on the other hand, the whole book is dominated by the thesis that " we mean by any concept nothing more than a set of operations." [22] We might naturally describe this thesis as experimental positivism, a description confirmed by the maxim that " experience is always described in terms of experience," [23] than which Berkeley, Comte, and Mill themselves could not be more positivistic.

After consideration of the issues at stake between the two views, it appears to me that the critical positivistic view of physical nature is much more probable than the metaphysical. The former can be stated more clearly and with fewer assumptions; the latter either generates artificial problems regarding the relations of mind and matter or else it fails to do justice to the experienced facts of mind as datum.

A further reason for preferring the positivistic to the metaphysical view is that the former can give a better account of the so-called secondary qualities than the latter. By secondary qualities are meant the colors, sounds, odors, and the like, which we constantly experience — in fact, all of the experienced qualities of things except their location in space, size, shape, and motion, which are called primary. For positivism, the primary and the secondary qualities both exist in nature, that is, in experience, although the physical sciences study the primary qualities apart from the secondary. But for the metaphysical view of physical nature, the real world beyond my experience has no color, sound, or odor such as we experience, but is only a system of moving particles. How these particles could generate our conscious experiences of the appropriate quality is an utter mystery.

Again, the set of facts which are described by the word " emergence " is more compatible with the positivistic than with the metaphysical view. In a word, emergence is the fact that new qualities, characters, or forms of life appear which have novel properties, not explicable in terms of the conditions out of which they arose. Consciousness of obligation, for example, is an emergent quality. It arose, doubtless, out of social situations, but the consciousness that I ought to do something is a new thing, totally different in kind from the fact that my family or my clan desires it to be done. Now, the metaphysical view of physical nature makes emergence utterly mysterious and unintelligible. How could physical matter engender moral obligation? The positivistic view, on the other hand, while it does not explain emergence, at least leaves the door open for a metaphysics that can make emergence more understandable.[24]

Again, science is becoming skeptical of its own mechanistic presuppositions. Max Planck writes that the development of physics has led us " away from the mechanical conception generally." [25] P. W. Bridgman confesses that " many will discover in themselves a longing for mechanical explanation which has all the tenacity of original sin," but, as a longing for exclusively mechanical explanation, this " is unjustifiable." [26] R. S. Lillie renews the suggestion often made by Royce and others that the apparently rigid mechanical laws of nature are but a statistical regularity, and that " ultramicroscopic phenomena . . . give evidence of an ultimate indetermination, . . . *i.e.,* of control by individual action." [27] Claude Bernard's *Experimental Medicine* holds to determinism in biology but refers the ultimate determination of life to the metaphysical world in which freedom is possible.[28] Now, these tendencies in science do not unambiguously point away from a metaphysical and toward a positivistic view of nature; they may only indicate a radical change in the character of scientific metaphysics. But at least they indicate that the pure mechanism of much modern science is on the wane [29] and that a new metaphysics is being shaped. Moreover, the indetermination and freedom of which we are now hearing is more characteristic of mind than of physical matter as we have known it, so that the newer

views are at least readily compatible both with a positivistic view of nature and with an idealistic metaphysics.

But it is in accounting for ideals that a materialistic
metaphysics is weakest and a positivistic view of physical
science most reasonable. So important is this consideration that it will be reserved for discussion in the next
chapter.

III

For the reasons given, and for many other reasons, the
positivistic view of physical nature seems preferable to
the metaphysical. By nature, as the object of the sciences, then, we mean simply the fact and the laws of actual and ideally possible experience. But this does not
yet solve the problem with which we started about the
fate of ideals in the universe. In fact, some believe that
the positivistic view of science makes any speculation
about the universe — that is, any metaphysics — impossible. We are thus driven to the second of the questions
raised at the outset of this chapter, namely: Is nature, the
object of the sciences, all that there is, or all that can be
known? May we know more about reality than scientific
method can discover?

With full recognition of the achievements of scientific
method, it cannot be denied that there is a widespread
uneasiness about what even so scientific a thinker as
R. B. Perry has called " The Cult of Science." [30]   C. E.
Ayres writes of " Science: the false Messiah," [31]   Arthur
Lynch of " Science: Leading and Misleading," [32] and

Hugo Dingler of " The Collapse of Science." [33]   In one or two of these writers there may be a certain journalistic striving for effect; but they are all trained in scientific methods, and they all agree that extravagant and misleading claims have been made in behalf of science.   That science is a true account of certain aspects of experienced facts no one doubts.   But that it tells or aims to tell the whole truth about experience as a whole may be questioned.   The present unrest about science challenges us to inquire whether nature as known by the sciences truly is all that can be known.

One way to go about answering that question is to consider what science presupposes at the start.   First of all, science has to presuppose mind, individual and social. Even the psychological sciences must do that.   If our view be true, mind is datum, and science cannot help presupposing it.   But no other mind than my own is immediately present to my experience, and so psychology has to presuppose other minds.   Likewise, the physical sciences, based as they are on experiment and observation, have to presuppose the minds of experimenters and observers.   Science, however " objective " it may be, is produced by human minds, and is no more or less trustworthy than the minds which produce it.[34]   Yet scientists like to ignore this fact; like to think of facts, of experiments, and of verifications, as though they occurred in a purely objective, nonmental realm.   An incident from personal experience may illustrate this point.   A distinguished experimental psychologist once exhibited a pulse tracing made by a sphygmograph with the comment, " Here is something more certain than all of your philosophical speculations. Here is a fact." The reply was, " Yes, but a mind has to tell what it means." The learned psychologist then made the undignified confession, " That is the dickens of it." [35]

Every science, even psychology, is a special perspective or view of the total range of the possible experience of minds. As abstract thought, all scientific hypothesis is mental activity; all experiment, in its immediate essence, is observation by a mind of its experiences under conditions controlled by the mind; and all verification involves interpretation by a mind of the results of successful experiments. At every moment the mind is present in the situation, and this, whether our theory of mind as datum be accepted or rejected. Hence, the results of every science need to be seen in relation to the mind as a whole, for the mind has many experiences and interests besides the scientific, such as the moral, the esthetic, the religious, and the philosophical.

In particular, when it presupposes mind, science must presuppose values and ideals. In so far as the experiencing of values and ideals is a fact, that fact falls, it is true, within the domain of the psychical sciences. But not any psychical, much less any physical, science can give an account of what values and ideals are worth realizing, or ought to be realized. Science would be impossible if the validity of ideals of reason (such as are embodied in mathematics and logic) were not presupposed; nay more, it would be impossible if some sort of " I ought to be loyal to the facts and to find their explanation " did not actuate the scientist. Observation and experiment can never prove or disprove the validity of ideals or values. They may prove that certain ideals can be realized, while others cannot be; they may prove that certain values are prized by the majority of men, while others are despised; but when the inference is drawn that therefore certain ideals and values ought to be striven for, one is in a different realm from that investigated by the sciences of nature. It matters little whether you call the investigation of the validity of ideals by the name of philosophy or normative sciences or ideal sciences; at any rate, you are raising problems which have no place in the natural sciences, physical or psychical, although the natural sciences have to presuppose certain ideals in order to be scientific, and scientists have to presuppose still other ideals in order to be human.

A further presupposition of science concerns its method. In general, the sciences have used the analytic method, the method of analyzing complex wholes into simple parts and studying the laws of the relations of these parts. In biology, psychology, and sociology this method is less satisfactory than in physics and chemistry; but even in physics it is coming to be recognized as not wholly adequate.[36] In addition to a complete analysis and synthesis of data, it is evident that a view of the object as a whole is necessary, for wholes often have properties which their parts do not have. A painting as a whole has a

beauty which none of its parts possesses; indeed, the more
minutely perfect the analysis of the painting, the less of the
beauty of the whole appears in the isolated part. Hence,
a synoptic or organic method must supplement and interpret the analytic.

As has been said, science usually has presupposed the
analytic method, but is tending more and more toward the
synoptic. Yet if science were to become completely
synoptic and consider all aspects of experience as a whole
in relation to all the results of analysis, it would then have
lost its character as science and have become philosophy.
In other words, as long as science remains science it must
remain abstract in the sense of cutting off its field from
completely organic relations to other fields of experience.
It presupposes analytic method as its special instrument;
utilizes synoptic method to a limited extent; and thus implies the need of a genuinely complete synoptic philosophy,
which shall try to interpret the meaning of experience as
a whole.

Whether natural science be properly regarded as metaphysical or as positivistic, science must make certain
presuppositions about what we call metaphysical reality.
If we interpret science as metaphysical, we must start, as
we find Bridgman doing, from the uncritical common sense
view of the external world, which, in its philosophical form
is usually called naturalism or physical realism. That is
a large presupposition to start with. If it be a mere un-
proved and unexamined presupposition, as it seems to be,
it cannot be said to be proved by science; it can only be

said to be assumed. But someone ought to inquire whether this materialistic assumption is correct. That someone is the philosopher. Even the metaphysical view of science, then, presupposes the need of philosophy.

The positivistic view, which involves less assumption on the part of science and therefore is described by E. W. Hobson as " an emancipatory movement," even more evidently than the metaphysical view of science, presupposes the need of philosophy. For if, as Hobson says, " physical realism is an otiose opinion," [37] it follows, as we have seen, that nature is the object of experience, and no more. That is, to be more precise, nature is for the sciences the system of actual and ideally possible perceptions of human beings. If science is confined to this realm, then the problems which science does not solve or even touch become most pressing. Man cannot rationally interpret his experience on the supposition that human experience is all that there is. Human experience must belong to a larger universe, and can be understood only when seen in relation to that universe. That universe must be such as to produce in us or cause to appear to us all of the phenomena of nature including all of our value experiences. But science does not reveal to us what that universe, that metaphysical power, is. Hence, the positivistic view of science drives us beyond the problem of science to the problem of philosophy: What is that whole of which our experience is a part, what is that reality of which science studies the appearances? Science, then, whatever our view of it, presupposes philosophy, since nature, as described by science, is not the whole of reality.

IV

We have been undertaking in this chapter to consider
what is meant by nature. The task has not been easy, and
it is not certain that a satisfactory answer to our questions
has been found. But so much is certain: that the sciences
— physical and psychological — which deal with nature
do not tell us all that we need to know about human experience. A mind means more than the natural sciences
can discover about it. Science is, of course, true, but it is
not the whole truth. Science is neither all knowledge nor
no knowledge. Science, then, needs to be supplemented by
a philosophy which rests, as Hugo Dingler puts it, on " the
old Greek idea of the unity of the spirit." [38]

In particular, it behooves us, in the light of our reflections on mind and nature, to raise again the question about
the meaning and place of ideals in the universe. To this
task the following chapter will be devoted.

CHAPTER III

IDEALS

Thus far we have started with mind as datum and have built up a view of the whole mind and of nature. In comparison with either the whole mind or nature, the datum-mind seems utterly insignificant. Yet this does not mean, as some idealists as well as misinterpreters of idealism hold, that the realm of immediate experience is unreal or unimportant.[1] Unless immediate experience — which is all we ever actually have and are — be both real and important, we have no basis for inference and no reason for anything. The datum-mind contains the clews to the spirit and meaning of reason. It is truly mind. Science and philosophy both are concerned with no other questions than what arise out of it. Yet it is surely not the whole universe nor even the whole mind. Present experience is much too fragmentary and too self-contradictory to be regarded as a complete cosmos in itself. Human experience, therefore, implies a universe beyond itself, to which it somehow belongs, with which it is closely related, and of which it can know something.

How, then, do we move from present experience to a universe? Is it not by the mind's power of framing ideals? Many thinkers hold this function of ideals to be of fundamental importance for our whole understanding of the world. Others admit it grudgingly, if at all.[2] Here is the old conflict between empiricist and rationalist, realist and idealist. It is the thesis of this chapter that ideals are not only practically important for the conduct of life but also theoretically important for the understanding of reality.

I

Are ideals of fundamental importance in the universe? Their apparent status in experience seems to point to a negative conclusion. At first sight, they certainly seem fragile and transitory in the presence of the hard facts. The real world is not ideal. Instead of harmony there is conflict. Mind and nature are in conflict with each other. Physical nature is constantly interfering with itself. There is conflict among minds and within minds. This is not only true naturally but also, so to speak, artificially. That is, not only do our natural tendencies and desires clash with each other, but also our philosophies of life are at war. So true is this at the present time that some writers are expressing themselves in terms of despair. One need not appeal to Spengler's *Downfall of the West*,[3] for evidence of such pessimism. Thoroughly healthy-minded writers do not hesitate to paint a dark picture. M. C. Otto, for instance, declares that " one of the marked characteristics of the time is the lack of any kind of total view." [4] Even a man like Hugo Dingler, who believes that the unity of the spiritual life is the legitimate aim of philosophy, says that " today all unity is lost." [5]

Now, this lack of unity would not disturb anyone and would scarcely be mentioned were it not for the ideal of unity which commands us to seek what we do not have and the imperative claims of which no mind true to itself can wholly deny. Our very unrest and confusion is a tribute to the rights of ideals. Indeed every conflict in human life, whatever else it may involve, is a conflict of ideals. No physical suffering would trouble us if we did not have the ideal of free and painless activity. Physical suffering does not distress us appreciably if undergone in the pursuit of an ideal which is sufficiently prized. A mere conflict of forces, whatever or wherever the forces were, would have no interest to us if in no way they furthered or hindered the realization of our ideals.

Ideals are of many kinds — high and low, spiritual and sensual, clear and vague, rational and irrational. Actual ideals, therefore, certainly conflict with each other, and seem to strive for the mastery of man's mind. This is indeed a tragic aspect of life, for ideals are principles of unity and organization, and yet they work toward disunity and disorganization. What true and high ideals are and how they are to be distinguished from false and low ones is not by any means obvious. *That* there are ideals is much more certain than *what* they are or ought to be; and that they conflict with each other is as certain as that they are.

Yet, in spite of the great importance of ideals, it is surprising how little attention has been paid by psychologists and philosophers to the problem of ideals as a distinct problem. Much has been written on values, but values and ideals are not identical. The normative sciences of logic, ethics, esthetics, and philosophy of religion have all dealt more or less with certain ideals. But the general problem of ideals has been strangely neglected. Among the significant studies of the subject from the psychological and educational standpoint is P. F. Voelker's *The Function of Ideals and Attitudes in Social Education*,[6] which has been made a basis of further researches by investigators under the guidance of W. S. Athearn. E. D. Starbuck is carrying on important experiments at the Research Station in Character Education at the University of Iowa. Many kinds of "personality tests" and "character tests" are being devised.[7]

But these tests are almost wholly from the point of view of the actual functioning of moral and religious ideals, and hence are subject to a threefold limitation. First, they are descriptive rather than normative, that is, they determine what is without considering critically what ought to be. The abundant work that has been done in the fields of history of morals and the evolution of ideals belongs in the same category. Such descriptive work is necessary, but it is not sufficient. Secondly, these investigations are restricted in their scope by their predominantly practical and educational interest, which tends to push important theoretical considerations into the background. Thirdly, the ideals thus far investigated have been almost wholly those of character (individual and social) and of religion. Hence it may be said that the problem of ideals as a whole has hardly been grasped by psychological and educational investigators.

The philosophers have paid more attention to the problem, but Kant used the word " ideal " in a technical sense, which tended to restrict the field of investigation.[8] Windelband and Rickert, and more recently Spranger, have been aware of the scope of the problem and have treated of ideals as " norms " or " forms of life," but their work has not received the attention outside Germany which is its due.   Perry has written *The Present Conflict of Ideals*,[9] but the limitations of that study are evident from its subtitle, *A Study of the Philosophical Background of the World War*. M. C. Otto's *Things and Ideals* [10] is a charming and vigorous defense of a pragmatic and social view of ideals but deals sketchily and in a somewhat too magisterial manner with views the author does not accept. He objects to the conception of philosophy as " a total vision of the universe," thus sweeping aside with a phrase the work of practically the whole history of philosophy as well as the heart of religious experience, on the ground that universality of knowledge is unattainable.   He even objects to seeking a view of the universe " which shall be as coherent and complete as we can obtain." [11]   This sounds like refusing to do our best and seems difficult to justify without more cogent proof than the author has given.

It may be that James Iverach goes too far when he says that "the study of ideals can hardly be said to have been begun." [12]   But it is clear that much remains to be

done, in theory as well as in practice, if we are to rescue
ideals from the chaos of tradition and convention, instinct
and desire, prejudice and fancy, in which they are now
confused.[13] Our present study cannot be a complete
theory. Any complete theory of ideals is at present impossible, and even if it were possible, could not be formulated
adequately in a single chapter. But the problems can
be defined and some suggestions offered toward possible
solutions.

II

What, then, do we mean by ideals? We may well consider one or two recently proposed definitions. Voelker
bases his investigation on a definition worked out by a
faculty committee at Teachers College, which reads as
follows:

" An ideal is probably best thought of as consisting of (I)
a generalized notion or general concept used as a plan or
standard of action, (II) the recognition and appreciation of
the practical worth of this plan or standard, and (III) a tendency (habit) to accept and obey the plan or standard, to act
it out in conduct. Unless these three elements are present we
cannot properly employ the term *ideal*." [14]

This is a suggestive definition. It states admirably the
attitude of practical idealism. Yet it raises certain questions. Are all ideals actually used and habitually obeyed?
Does not the assumption that they are thus used and
obeyed create too wide a gap between " ideals " and the
standards which men acknowledge without obeying?

Further, is it true that all ideals are plans of action? Perhaps, in some sense. Yet is it not confusing to put a reference to action into a definition which, if it is to cover all ideals, must include ideals of appreciation and of thought as well as of conduct? The Teachers College definition covers only ideals of action which are actually acted on. Are there no other ideals than these?

Another definition, proposed by W. D. Niven,[15] runs as follows: An ideal is

" a conception of what, if attained, would fully satisfy; of what is perfect of its kind, and, in consequence, is the pattern to be copied, and the standard by which actual achievement is to be judged."

This definition is not restricted to ideals of action, but it, like that of Teachers College, holds that the ideal is the perfect and complete. But do we not often have ideals which are low and imperfect, and which we know are low and imperfect? We need a realistic, thoroughly unsentimental view of ideals. Is it not more realistic to grant that there are low ideals on which we do act and high ones on which we do not act, than to preclude these daily human experiences by definition?

If we were to build a revised definition in the light of the merits and defects of those considered, it would read somewhat like this: *An ideal is a general concept of a type of experience which we approve.* The multiplication table, the concept of love, and a sonnet scheme are thus ideals. They are ideals if we approve of them, whether we seek to realize them or not and whether we regard

them as perfect or not. The schoolboy may approve of
the multiplication table, yet refuse to try to discover the
cost of the carpet for a room 29 2/3 feet wide and 31 7/8
feet long, if the carpet costs $2.25 a yard. His recogni-
tion of his ideal may be undimmed and unaffected by his
refusal to realize it. Or it is possible to acknowledge the
ideal of love, and yet in practice to hate very effectively.
Or we may approve of the sonnet scheme in principle, yet
fail to write a sonnet. Again, our lower self may approve
what our better self condemns.

From our definition all reference to emotion is purposely omitted, save such emotional quality as is implied
in approval.[16] It is doubtless true that worthy ideals
should arouse deep emotion. We should not only approve, but approve whole-heartedly and with feeling.
But if all ideals were necessarily accompanied by such
emotion, the practical problems of life would be at once
simpler and more complex than they are now. True and
false ideals would both be better loved and better realized
than at present. But as human nature is, it is much easier
to teach persons an ideal than to teach them to feel appropriate emotions toward it. It is quite possible to recognize an ideal, and yet, without feeling any emotional at-
tachment to it, to choose some conflicting ideal as the
guide of life.

Our definition may be tested by considering its implications. Its first and most obvious implication is that, as a
generalized concept, an ideal is visible only to thought.
It cannot be perceived in sense experience. We may find

in sense experience instances of objects which we call
ideally perfect. A perfect tree is possible. But that tree
is not the ideal itself; other perfect trees might be very
different from that one. Hence when we say of any object that it is, in any sense, ideal, we are measuring our
present experience by a generalized concept, which
thought alone can grasp. This thought is present in
Schwarz's description of religion as *das Ungegebene,*
" what is not given." [17]

Secondly, since an ideal is a general concept of a type
of experience, it may be regarded as implying an hypothesis about future experience. If and when we have experience of the type described, the ideal asserts that we
shall then approve it. If the actual experience which
conforms to the ideal elicits the same approval as it did
in the ideal, to that extent the hypothesis is verified. But
too often the castle in Spain, when constructed, proves
not to be habitable. Plumbing is poor and taxes high.

Thirdly, an ideal is a principle of unity. Any general
concept, whether we approve it or not, is of course a principle of unity, for it organizes many particulars under one
universal. To say " brick " unifies life wonderfully: how
complex it would be to give each individual brick a name
of its own! But an ideal goes further, for it unifies our
experiences in relation to our approvals. And the more
actively ideals are pursued and realized, the more systematic may this unification become; for our ideals are so
related to each other and to experience that a system of
ideals is necessary.[18] Considering this trait of ideals in

relation to our view of mind in Chapter I, we may say that
every ideal is at least an incipient movement from the
datum-self to the whole-self. In its lowest terms, every
ideal is a vision of some sort of possible whole of experience, some organization of the life of mind.

It follows that, fourthly, an ideal is a principle of control and selection. An ideal which is merely conceived
and not acted on is, of course, only a control of attention
and a selection of possibilities for approval. But a functioning ideal, at work toward the unification of experience,
controls experience concretely. Sometimes that control,
when happily exercised by one who loves the ideal, is as
effortless and perfect as the flight of a bird. More often
that control is a struggle incompletely successful. But
control does not necessarily imply resistance to the control; it implies only the guidance of experience toward a
goal.

An ideal is, fifthly, a plan of action. The Teachers
College definition was right in this assumption, wrong
only in leaving so ambiguous a term undefined in a definition. If by action we mean merely biological behavior,
not all ideals are plans of action. But if by action we
mean the organization of any series of experiences with
reference to a purpose, then an ideal is always a plan of
action. Sometimes the action involved in the realization
of an ideal is not evident. Yet just as apparent physical
rest but conceals the motions of invisible atoms, thus an
ideal may be so steadily realized as to produce the illusion
of inactivity. Indeed, it is possible that this steadiness

may become an habitual attitude like obstinacy, and be a
foe to creative and progressive activity; even so, this en-
crusted and irrational ideal functions as a principle of
action, but the wrong kind of action. Every ideal, therefore, is an *Aufgabe*, a problem or task. Since experience
is apparently inexhaustible, an ideal may also be described
in terms applied by Kant to the world of experience as
eine unendliche Aufgabe, an infinite task. Any ideal,
even the lowest, calls on us to do more than can be completed in any finite time.

An ideal has often been spoken of as a goal or end
($\tau\epsilon\lambda os$), but this should not be taken to mean that an
ideal prescribes a certain fixed point as the stopping-place
of action. On the contrary, the true ideal bids us to realize the approved type in every possible aspect of experience. Let us suppose that friendship is the ideal in question. It would be manifest treason to the ideal to say,
" Now that a friendship has been formed, the ideal is
realized, and so we have reached the end of friendship."
Or if truth be the ideal, how suicidal it would be to say,
" Now that a truth is known, we have attained the ideal,
and there is nothing more to be done about truth." The
ideal, rather, implies that there shall always be more
friendship, always more truth. It is clearly a principle
of action, and of diversified action.[19] The realization of
an ideal is both a process and a promise. The essence of a
living universe is " Excelsior " — higher! Always more.

In certain senses, an ideal is, sixthly, a social principle.
This is, however, not at once evident from the nature of

an ideal. The expression, " which *we* approve," is social
in form but individual in meaning. A concept is not an
ideal for me if I merely know it to be a type of experience
approved by others. It may be an object of interest;
perhaps a stone of stumbling and a rock of offense; but it
may lack entirely the quality of an ideal in my mind. I
may know that head-hunting is an ideal in the rural sec-
tions of Borneo without acknowledging it as an ideal for
me. Or I may know that violation of law is an ideal of
certain of my fellow citizens without myself holding it as
an ideal. I may even reject the ideals of my own group.
An ideal, in its essence, seems to be individual rather than
social. Approval by a person is necessary to the very existence of an ideal, although that acknowledgment may be
implicit and in attitude only, rather than explicit and
verbal.

Nevertheless ideals are social. In our study of mind,
we found that mind is not fully intelligible unless understood in relation to its environment. Every mind stands
in social relations, and its ideals are formed in those social
relations. The individual has a share — a more important share and responsibility than many social theorists
will grant — but the individual cannot form ideals without using the materials given him by his fellows. Society
has had some part in the forming of the most individualistic, eccentric, and anarchistic of ideals: the antisocial
egoist could not have formed his pitiful ideal had he not
been in contact with society. Even the lowest ideals must
grow out of social soil and have some social reference.

And the higher, that is, the more reasonable and truth-loving, an ideal is, the more fully will it take society into account. Indeed the concept of society as worthy of our devotion is one of the most fundamental of ideals, and only the person capable of sustained intellectual imagination can ever grasp that ideal. Society is never our datum! Its great complexity of suffering and heroism, of pettiness and greatness, is too vast for any mind to apprehend in full detail.[20] All ideals are, in a sense, social; but few ideals are intelligently and adequately social.

An ideal, seventhly, may be called a principle of love. Here, again, is an aspect not clearly revealed in the definition. Yet the ideal is something which is acknowledged as worthy of approval; and approval is at least a mild form of love. An ideal of any sort is a yearning that is akin to love. In every ideal there is at least a dim love of power, of unity, of truth, or of other persons.[21] But if it be true that the ideal is a principle of *love,* it is also of the utmost theoretical (and practical) importance to remember that love is an *ideal* principle, and hence subject in some sense to the laws of judgment. Ideal love is not fleeting desire.

We have said that an ideal is visible only to thought, is an hypothesis about future experience, is a principle of unity, of control, selection, and action, a social principle, and a principle of love. But it must be clearly borne in mind that an ideal is not a value. A value is an actually realized ideal or an ideal in process of realization. It is the experience which exists when an ideal is acted on, is obeyed, and conformed to. The ideal is the plan; the value is the construction in accordance with the plan. The ideal is the pattern; the value is the product which conforms to the pattern.

III

It is always easier to state a general principle than to apply it to the organization of particular facts. General principles are exceedingly useful, indeed are necessary, if there are to be either ideals or science; but they attain their special usefulness by omitting the concrete detail of the facts and considering only the traits which many facts possess in common. This process has been well described by C. D. Burns. "Abstraction is logical forgetfulness or the art of forgetting; and it is not misleading unless you forget that you have forgotten." [22] Hence a didactic old-fashioned Sunday School story book is easier to write than a poem or a great novel or a history. Didactic literature and history remember the concrete facts and relations of experience, which the Sunday School story book forgets in its interest in the moral. If the abstract moral is to be effective, the concrete fable must be rich in details and true to life.

Let us then draw closer to the facts from which our abstract definition of ideals has been derived. We face seemingly hopeless confusion. The one ideal which stands out as true is embodied in the maxim that one man's meat is another man's poison. But if we leave the struggle of ideals to the law of evolution and let the fittest survive, we arrive at a strange result; for ideals of love and of hate, of war and of peace are, by this test, equally fit. They have survived. This confusion is a problem; but the mind obstinately believes that problems have solutions. Not even the confusion of ideals need baffle investigation.

If our definition be correct, the confusion seems to be even greater than is commonly believed, for it includes in its scope both the perfect and the imperfect, the highest and the lowest ideals. Yet it seems sheer sentimentalism to deny that low ideals are ideals. Not only do men seek and approve low aims, but human nature is so illogical that the same man may in different moods entertain a high ideal and a low one which conflicts with it; he may even obstinately assert two incompatible ideals at the same time. This aspect of the problem, however, we shall not consider just now.

Our definition enlarges the realm of the ideal by making it include far more than is commonly included in it. We may — to select only the more important — speak of ideals of character, of science, of the esthetic, of religion, and of philosophy.

Ideals of character undoubtedly occupy a unique place, for without some traits of a good character no worthy ideal of any sort can be realized. Character is a function of will as temperament is of the affective life. Without a good will, every ideal fails. It is as necessary to science as it is to religion, as necessary to art as it is to social welfare. It is not merely true that actual character is essential if ideals are to be realized; it is also true that the ideal of character is a constituent part of all other ideals. The approval of any type of experience would logically include the approval of character, that is, of a will loyal to at least that ideal. This is related to Kant's doctrine of the primacy of the practical reason.[23]

Less obvious, but theoretically of very great importance, is the ideal nature of science. Some will at once object to speaking of sciences as consisting of, or as involving, ideals. They will say that science has to do with facts, not with ideals; that a scientist may be a bad man morally, without esthetic taste, or religious principles, or philosophical perspective — if only he describes the facts in accordance with scientific method. If only! That exception is necessary, and it brings the most unwilling scientist back into a corner of the idealistic fold. However scornful or indifferent a scientist might be toward other ideals — and there are some scientists as intolerant of art, for example, as some esthetic fanatics are of science — he cannot be a scientist without scrupulous loyalty to the scientific ideal. He approves such types of experience as observation and experiment, description and explanation. They are his ideals. If a highly technical scientific purist should object that the word " approval " brings in an unscientific element and that he does not " approve " scientific method, but merely uses it, such an objection would be groundless; for what is better evidence of approval than use? If anyone thinks that a scientist does not regard scientific method as an ideal, let him contemplate how a scientist feels about a person who pretends to use scientific method without adequate training or skill.

If we look into the details of scientific method, we find its ideal character confirmed. Cassirer says that " no physicist experiments and measures with the particular instrument that he has sensibly before his eyes; but he substitutes for it an ideal instrument in thought, from which all accidental defects, such as necessarily belong to the particular instrument, are excluded." [24] Similarly, Planck, speaking of the special problem of reversible processes, says that that problem is " hardly a question of actual experiments and an actual physicist, but of ideal processes, so-called ideal experiments and an ideal physicist, who applies all experimental methods with absolute accuracy," and he speaks of " the trust displayed in ideal experiments by the theorist in physical chemistry." Planck remarks in another connection that " we mean by ' world ' nothing but the ideal picture of the future." [25] If, then, science consists of ideal scientists in an ideal laboratory with ideal instruments, dealing with an ideal world, a scientist who is skeptical of idealism is a strange self-contradiction. All ideals are clews to a world beyond itself which the mind follows in answering the question, " What do I, the datum-mind, mean? " [26] Without acknowledgment of ideals as such clews, science could never be, and the blind confusion of experience would remain blind confusion.

Experience of the beautiful also implies ideals. It is true that esthetic ideals seem sometimes to be in constant flux. Of all the ideals, they seem to be most affected by conventions and to differ most widely in different civilizations. What constitutes the essence of esthetic pleasure, what experience of the beautiful is, has not yet been put into words which clarify and enlighten the mind. Yet when we speak of beauty, we surely mean some sort of satisfying and unified harmony. Every beautiful object, sound, or person somehow conforms to this ideal.

Yet the satisfaction need not be, and in many cases is not, properly described as mere pleasure. An experience is often deeply moving and even in a sense painful, yet satisfying through its harmony and wholeness. Moritz Geiger well distinguishes between the surface-effect and the depth-effect of art.[27] Some beauty merely pleases or amuses; this is surface-effect. Other beauty moves the whole personality through and through; this is depth-effect. Surface-effect is what is called " mere " pleasure; depth-effect is something nobler — happiness. From Geiger's view we may infer that surface-effect is thoughtless, while depth-effect is precisely such a total organization of experience as the greatest philosophers have called thought and reason. How to define or create or express beauty remains a mystery which words are inadequate to describe; yet, once created, true beauty is an embodiment of the ideal of reason. It is a unique embodiment, not identical with science or religion or philosophy; but it belongs to the one republic of ideals. Each state in that republic is autonomous; yet each state is subject to the federal constitution of reason.

That religion is another state within the republic of

ideals is the testimony of the history of the human race.
So true is this that any reference to ideals is often condemned by the pagan man-on-the-street as too religious
for him.   Religion is essentially the organization of life
with reference to faith in and worship of some divine invisible spiritual being or beings.   Faith in God is an assertion that the highest ideal is real in some sense,[28] in spite
of the fact that that ideal is not and cannot be fully
realized in mind and nature as we experience them.
Hence, the religious ideal, which calls us to contemplation
of the highest and cooperation with his purposes, is, like
the esthetic and the scientific, an integral part of the total
ideal of reason.   It is an essential part; neither science
nor art nor character nor any other experience or activity
can usurp the place of religion without the mutilation of
reason.   But it is only a part.   Although religion is an attitude toward the whole of life, a vision of its ideal meaning and holiness, yet religion is not itself the whole of life.
Although it is in a more intimate relation to the whole
than is any single state to the political republic of which
it is a part, and the political analogy is therefore misleading at this point, yet it is subject to the constitution.   The
ideal of religion is part of the system of ideals and thus
belongs to reason, the spirit and judge of all system; just
as the realization of religion belongs to the system of
values, and, thus again, to reason.

This leads us to the ideal of the complete system of all
ideals, which we call reason or philosophy.   There is, we
have seen, something about the nature of the mind which

refuses to let us dwell on mere present facts alone; we are driven beyond the facts toward their meaning, beyond the datum toward its interpretation, indeed, beyond everything which we can regard as a part or as incomplete toward the whole in which the parts find their place and the incomplete its completion. The striving toward complete unity is reason.

We started in by defining the ideal as " a general concept of a type of experience which we approve." There will be those who will recall that definition, and, applying it to the notion of reason or philosophy as an ideal, will ask, " Is this, then, what ' reason ' reduces to? After all, is it only what I approve? This must mean that your philosophy and your reason are only a rationalization of desire! " In answer, we may extend Geiger's conception of surface-effect and depth-effect from the esthetic to the whole realm of ideals. What we desire on the surface of our lives may indeed have little relation to the *true* ideal. But what we approve, morally, scientifically, esthetically, religiously, rationally — in the light of our whole mind, our whole experience — must be the true ideal. Surface-effect is problem and starting-point; depth-effect is solution and completion of life. One is the datum-self; the other, the whole-self. A depth-effect which includes all that we can know of ourselves and our environment — social, physical, metaphysical — enlarges our ideas, criticizes and elevates our desires, and disciplines our approvals. It is not that the ideal is whatever we now like; but rather that we learn to like what is truly ideal. Be-

ginning with approvals based on sensuous desires, we are
driven to approvals based on truth.   The desire for truth
is also a desire; but it is a desire which has a right to
challenge and to reorganize all other desires.   Thus we
have moved from our first definition of ideals, which was
purely descriptive, toward a more normative definition,
which would read as follows: *An ideal is a general concept
of a type of experience which we approve in relation to a
complete view of all our experience, including all our
approvals.*

It is often held at the present time that reason has to
do with the means, but not with the ends of life.   Nature
gives us our desires; let science tell us how to attain
them.[29]   This is an extreme reaction against " Puritanism."   But, if taken literally, this view is the collapse of
civilization.   It is only if ideals are rational that the ends
of human striving are sane.   But if ideals are irrational,
if every impulsive desire is to be treated as on the same
level, no scientific technique in attaining irrational ends
will ever rescue the world from chaos.   Reason calls us
to see our minds and our world as a whole; and to approve
as ideal only those ends which are rational in the light of
that vision.

IV

The ideal, as we have found, is what makes possible
knowledge of our own minds and of nature, and, above all,
any contemplation of truth as a whole.   It is what gives
meaning to both liberty and law; it is the meaning of

every meaning. Yet there remains the substantial fact
that mind and nature are, as we have seen, at war within
and between themselves. Ideals seem to be alien to the
impersonal and unfeeling facts. We have found that
several different kinds of fundamental ideals are implied
by the facts of human experience; yet, often surface-
effect seems to triumph over depth-effect in human minds,
and nature over both. But despite the conflict between
the ideal and the real, it is impossible to give up either
one without also giving up the other. To give up the real
(if that form of words means anything) would be to give
up all basis for ideals and all possibility of their realization. To give up the ideal would be to give up our very
reason for belief in and thought about the real. For,
without ideals, no science; without science, no knowledge
of the real.[30] Ideal and real: each needs the other, yet
each seems to oppose the other.

But the assertion that the real necessitates the ideal
may give us pause. What right have we to expect that
the real shall conform to our ideals? Yet it cannot be
denied that knowledge of the real as anything more than
the moment's experience is possible only through scientific and logical ideals. Moreover the real, as immediately
given in the datum-mind, always shows a tendency to the
formation of ideals of some sort. On the other hand,
there appears to be no universal necessity which drives all
minds to the realization of the highest ideals. The logical
necessity of the logical ideal does not involve the psychological necessity of any mind's caring about it or obeying

it. The moral necessity of the moral ideal does not actually compel anyone to be good. From every side, then,
the problem of the realization of the ideal is acute.

The first and probably the most fundamental problem
connected with the realization of ideals is that of human
freedom. Apart from any formal definition or analysis of
freedom, all will agree that an act of intelligent choice
may properly be called a free act. Now, without free
acts in this sense, rational ideals can neither be formed
nor appropriated nor realized. It is true that the ideals
of primitive man are often mere group imitation of involuntary behavior or of accidental events. But depth-
effects cannot be wholly involuntary, for where the will is
not involved the full depth of human nature has not been
stirred. The will need not be regarded as the creator of
ideals; but without a free act of acknowledgment no ideal
can become my ideal. Logical thought does not occur in
minds which do not choose to think. Bowne has pointed
out more clearly than anyone else the fact that without
freedom the possibility of arriving at any distinction between truth and error is blotted out.

Freedom is thus essential to the formation of valid
ideals; how much more obviously is it necessary to their
realization! To carry out an ideal it is necessary to guide
a long series of acts so that it will conform to the approved
type. This implies a purpose, freely chosen and freely
sustained; the free choice of means to its attainment; and
the free will to criticize every stage of achievement in the
light of the chosen ideal.

The realization of ideals, then, rests on freedom. It also rests on another fact, which we have hitherto purposely not mentioned, namely, the fact that the higher ideals, those which stir depth-effects, are experienced as imperative. True ideals are principles of what ought to be.[31] They confront mind or nature as these are and either assert that they are as they ought to be (as when we correctly solve a mathematical problem) or that they are not as they ought to be (as when we make a discord or commit a sin).

But since the word " ought " is commonly used of situations which are ethical in the narrower sense of the word, rather than scientific or esthetic, it is commonly, but falsely, believed that science and art have no interest in the " ought." It is true that science, as science, does not care whether its results are esthetically satisfying or morally inspiring or religiously edifying or the reverse. Hence it is often said that science is *wertfrei* — free of all reference to values or ideals. But while science has no concern with *other* ideals, it is deeply, nay even passionately, concerned with its own ideal. The man of science ought to be well-informed, ought to use sound methods, ought to report his results accurately; and, more deeply, ought to measure every hypothesis by the facts and every fact by his hypotheses. I know that nature exists because I know that I ought to think in accordance with scientific ideals. I can and do distinguish between illusion and perception of " real " objects at bottom because I ought to be coherent. Many are not aware of this fact, and suppose that they make this distinction simply out of practical necessity; but practical necessity unguided by ideals would never construct a true scientific method or a true view of nature. These ensue only when we recognize an obligation to seek single-mindedly for truth.

Every true ideal, then, is imperative. It is not only "worthy of our approval," as we have said, but also binding on our will. It is what Windelband calls a "norm," a principle which one ought to obey.[32] This fact leads us to a further revision of our definition of ideals. The complete normative definition, the definition of true ideals which ought to be acknowledged and realized, would run as follows: *An ideal is a general concept of a type of experience which we approve in relation to a complete view of all our experience, including all our approvals, and which we acknowledge that we ought to realize.*

Yet there are differences among ideals as regards this imperative quality. We may speak of three classes of true ideals: the ought-to-be-and-must-be, the ought-to-be-and-may-be, and the ought-to-be-yet-cannot-be. Let us look at these somewhat more closely.

There is, first, the ought-to-be-and-must-be. These are the ideals which a mind ought to obey and must obey if it is to function as a mind at all. Such are the principles which compel us to recognize that the present datum is not all that there is, that we have had a past, that there are other persons, that there is an order of nature by which persons may communicate, and that moral obligation is binding. These, and other equally important ideals, may be called in Kantian language constitutive, for they make possible, they " constitute," the whole framework of an orderly structure of experience.

The second class of ideals is the ought-to-be-and-may-be. These are such ideals as should be obeyed and realized under certain conditions, yet are not essential to the very existence of orderly experience. We may or may not write poems; experience can exist without our verses; yet if we elect or are born to write them, we ought to conform to an esthetic ideal. The ought-to-be-and-may-be ideals, then, may be called not constitutive, but regulative. They do not make experience possible, but they regulate changes within experience.

The third class is that of the ought-to-be-yet-cannot-be. To be more precise, these ideals ought to be obeyed; the experiences which they describe ought to be sought, yet those experiences can never be fully realized. Some suppose that all ideals are of this kind. In a sense it is true that we can never say that we have finished fulfilling all that any ideal requires. Thus there is a curious relation between the ought-to-be-and-must-be and the ought-to-be-yet-cannot-be; for what, in this sense, must be, is precisely what we can never reasonably cease, and therefore can never finish, obeying. Yet in the case of the must-be we can apprehend what the ideal requires and can, if we have done our best, report it as completely fulfilled to date. But in the case of the cannot-be, we are unable either to apprehend fully what the ideal requires or, much less, to fulfil it completely. I may apprehend adequately that there are other persons, despite my ignorance of the details of their inner lives. But, to take the supreme ideal that cannot be, I cannot apprehend or fulfil what I mean by the ideal of perfection. As soon as perfection is defined, some artist will catch a glimpse of a perfection not included in the definition. As soon as a perfection is realized, it is merely a starting-point for new perfections. If the mind is an active and creative process, if ideals are principles of its activity, the very conception of a completed perfection is a self-contradiction. The more active and creative a mind, the more will its perfection expand. Perhaps democracy itself is another ideal that ought-to-be-yet-cannot-be.

If these things are true, the kingdom of the ideal is both in mind and in nature, both present and future, both necessary and contingent, both constitutive and regulative. We are beginning to see how fundamental ideals are in our experience.

V

Having surveyed the meaning and nature of ideals, we can now return to the question raised in Chapter I: What is the status of ideals in the universe? Leaving aside differences in detail, although some of them are very important, there are two chief answers to our problem, namely, the naturalistic and the idealistic.

The naturalistic answer holds that, apart from man,

nature is indifferent to ideals, and that human ideals —
although good for man — are purely human products in
a universe which itself is both impersonal and without
concern for ideals or their realization. Naturalism, it is
evident, is based on what, in Chapter II, was called the
metaphysical view of science. Naturalists differ in their
views about what ideals are best for man and how important those ideals are in man's adjustments to his fellows
and to nature; [33] but all of them agree that ideals have no
place in and no meaning for the universe apart from
human experience. The universe has no ideals and no
purposes; the universe cares for no values. It is just
what the natural and psychological sciences assert it to
be; just that, and no more, can be known.

Idealism, on the other hand, holds that ideals and
values are not merely human standards and human experiences, but that they reveal the objective structure,[34]
or, perhaps, the conscious purpose, of the universe, just
as human sense experience and human standards of scientific method reveal the laws of nature. As with naturalism, so with idealism there are many varieties and shades
of opinion (some of which will be discussed in a later
chapter). Indeed, I am now using idealism in so broad a
sense that it includes many views not ordinarily called
idealistic. There are metaphysical dualists, pluralists and
monists; persons whose view of the physical world is
quite realistic, such as scholastics and some critical realists; deists, theists, and pantheists; believers in all religions and in none; — all of whom fall, in this broad sense,

under the title of idealist. Many of them would dislike being called idealists, but they would agree with what is meant, objecting only to the word. All these " idealists " hold that goodness and truth and beauty are imperative ideals for the universe independent of man as well as for man, and that when man is seeking to realize them, he is working toward the very goals for which the universe is striving.[35] Our discussion of this problem will focus attention on those forms of naturalism and idealism which seem to be most important.

The issue at stake between naturalism and idealism concerns the meaning and dignity of man. Personal life and social institutions are profoundly affected by the truth of one or the other of these views. Some men hope that idealism is true; some hope that naturalism is true. Some fear lest naturalism may be true; but no one would be likely to fear lest idealism may be true, for idealism holds that the universe is on the side of man's deepest and best desires. Therefore it is most essential that our judgment may not be befuddled by our hopes and our fears. The *American Mercury* and the *Sunday School Times* are typical and habitual offenders against this principle. Too often not merely the popular interpreters but even the serious thinkers of both naturalism and idealism base their appeal on an attempt to play on the emotions. It may be that the desire to be in agreement with the Brahmins of the academic world may play as effective an emotional part as the desire for a front seat in the synagogue. The point to keep in mind is the fact that the appeal to emotion is equally irrelevant to logic, whoever makes it.

Emotion has a very great part in life; but that part is not to prove the truth of your principles nor to guide your reason.

Hence the merely practical arguments which are urged on both sides are to be regarded with suspicion. If it be said that naturalism alone is truly social or that idealism alone is truly social, the statement may be true; but the social value of a belief does not prove its truth. Society must in the end conform to truth, not truth to society. We hear it said that naturalism destroys all hope and so makes ideals futile; or that it adds great incentives to ideal living, because this life is all, and hence everything depends on man's effort. Again, it is declared that idealism is false because it destroys all incentive by its view that the ideal is real, for this means that reality is perfect and improvement is both unnecessary and impossible; or, on the other hand, that idealism is true because it alone gives hope and courage for the work of social reform. Such arguments cancel each other; whether used by communists against religion or by the clergy for religion they are equally illogical as proof. What truth they contain is a practical application of a principle, but is no proof of that principle. Pragmatism, loosely applied, has created much confusion of this sort.

If, then, we ask what is the logical basis of the case for naturalism, it may be stated concisely under two heads. First, science appears to support a naturalistic view, and secondly, the origin and the development of ideals seem to point in the same direction.

Science reveals a world in which the beautiful and the

ugly, the good and the bad, are an outcome of precisely the same forces and laws. The electron knows and cares nothing about the rainbow which it helps to constitute; much less is it concerned with the human experience of the rainbow's beauty. Furthermore nature, as investigated by science, is very unideal; evil and suffering abound. This argument has made a profound impression on the modern world and has shaken the confidence of many idealists.

The other naturalistic argument has to do with the origin and nature of ideals. Ideals are said to be derived from the tribal *mores*, from social customs and conventions, from inherited tendencies, and from the behavior of the organism in adjustment to environment. There is little reason to suppose that such origins would reveal the objective structure of reality. They reveal social prejudices and biological wants. No more! It is ridiculous to suppose that our prejudices and wants are eternal laws.

These arguments are in the ascendancy in many quarters today, but they are far from convincing. They are based on the assumption that science is metaphysical truth, and it was shown in Chapter II how precarious that assumption is, and how much more probable is the alternative " positivistic " view of science.

But there are two objections to naturalism apart from this which seem to me to be fatal. In the first place, naturalism overlooks the fact that natural science is not the whole of experience and does not even take full ac-

count of it. Besides science, there are beauty and goodness and holiness. The scientific attitude toward these
is to describe their causes and their effects, abstracting
from, that is, forgetting, their ideal meaning and value.
This is part of what Robert Shafer means when he says
that " the trouble with naturalism is that it wholly neglects the facts of experience which characterize us as
human beings in order to emphasize other facts which
link us to the animal and inorganic worlds." [36] A true
philosophy must take its stand on all of the facts, on the
whole datum, not trying to explain anything away, as
naturalism explains the meaning of ideals away. In the
second place, the results of science cannot be used to refute the objective validity of ideals, for science itself, as
we have seen, rests on the validity of ideals. What is
scientific method but an ideal? Does it not, then, involve
the principle of a system of ideals? We have found, indeed, that only on condition that some ideals can be
trusted can we get from the datum-self to any true
thought of our environment or of a world other than our
present experience.

If naturalism only asserted that some ideals are false
and some are true it would be telling us no news. But it
goes further and asserts that reality is indifferent to all
ideals. In so doing it contradicts itself; for unless reality
in some way embodies ideals akin to those of scientific
thought, science — even the science of behaviorism —
cannot be true, and naturalism has no standing ground.
But if reality truly conforms to ideals set up by scientific

thought, there is no reason, in principle, why it should not conform to the ideals of the good and the beautiful, as well as the scientifically true. Naturalism, then, is provincialism in thought; it consists in taking a part of man's idealizing thought for the whole. It pretends to rest on experience, yet it ignores a large part of experience. It pretends to rest on science, yet its logic would deny the ideals which make science possible. Like all provincialisms and narrow patriotisms, it is shortsighted and self-refuting. But men keep on believing in it, for the way of ideals is very hard and the apparent hostility of nature to ideals is evident.

Here we have put our finger on the weakness of the case for idealism — the apparent hostility of nature and the apparent weakness of ideals. Yet nature is not utterly hostile and ideals are not utterly weak. That ideals exist at all — that they grow again and again even when trampled on — shows that nature at least tolerates them. Nay more, they spring from the same soil as do our bodies and all living creatures. Hence the universe is not understood until ideals are understood; and it is to be understood by means of ideals. Our view of things must be such as to explain both nature and ideals and also the fact that nature is known through ideals, while ideals are imperfectly realized in nature.

The great idealist, Hegel, is often charged with dogmatism and obscurity. This charge is not without reason. Besides, it is an admirable defense-mechanism for those who would avoid the task of understanding Hegel. But even they will concede that Hegel appreciated fairly and stated clearly certain objections to idealism.

" Two popular fallacies," he says, " stand opposed to the reality of the rational: namely, the belief that ideas and ideals are nothing but chimeras and that philosophy is a system of such delusions and, secondly, the opposite belief that ideas and ideals are something far too excellent to have reality or far too weak to secure it for themselves." [37]

These views of the ideal, it is evident, *are* fallacies just because they fail to account for the relations that actually exist between nature and ideals. If all ideals are either chimerical or helplessly excellent, their power in interpreting nature is incomprehensible; their function in giving sanity and purpose to human life, unintelligible. Naturalism is based on some facts; idealism refutes it, not by denying those facts, much less by discounting science, but by pointing to other facts and other ideals with which science is allied, but from which it abstracts.

Idealism, then, is true because the real is known only through the ideal, and because the kingdom of ideals is the kingdom of reason. Idealism, as I see it, does not hold that all true ideals actually are realized. It does not even guarantee that all true ideals ever will be perfectly realized: the ought-to-be-yet-cannot-be may always continue unrealized. Absolute perfection may never be completed; the perfection of the universe may consist in its perfectibility. But idealism holds that ideals are the patterns according to which the universe is working as a society of free persons for the progressive realization of ideals. The universe is built for eternity; for long struggle, long pain, long disappointment; yet it is built for attaining ideal ends through all these bitter experiences, as well as through sweet ones.

Idealism believes that this view of life is truer to the facts than is naturalism; explains the existence of ideals and of value, our knowledge of nature through ideals, and the struggle between nature and ideals more reasonably than does naturalism. Idealism is the appeal from part-experience to whole-experience; from part-reason to whole-reason; from part-ideals to whole-ideals.

Thus the essence of the case for idealism is that the datum-mind is always more or less meaningless unless it be related to an ideal whole. Despite the importance of knowing facts, no fact by itself is of any importance. A mere collection of facts, blindly chosen, has no importance for theory or practice, until a mind begins to see in the facts a meaning, a law, or an ideal which the facts somehow embody or can be made to serve. Facts in relation to ideals are the source of all meaning. In the Upanishads it is written that " the wise in heart found the roots of what is in what is not." Facts, in other words, find their meaning in ideals which are not present facts, but are none the less real.

If, then, this idealism be true, we have an entirely new perspective. The struggle between nature and ideals — so distressing to the " tender-minded " idealist made famous by William James — must itself reveal an ideal, a part of the purpose of the universe. Struggle, progress, new creation; these happen in nature. But they happen slowly and with much suffering. " My lord delayeth his coming." The kingdom, ever coming, does not arrive.

What, then, shall the idealist think of nature? — for he must think of it as fully and as objectively as does the naturalist. Nature is a vehicle for the realization and for great difficulty in the realization of ideals; and the idealist, if his view be true, must find a meaning in frustration as well as in attainment. He must have iron in his soul, and say, The iron is good. To be an idealist, then, requires a great deal of courage.

VI

Naturalism emphasizes the weakness of ideals, and idealism their security. Ideals are indeed both weak and secure. Naturalism provides only for their weakness, and calls on man to make the best he can of it. Idealism, with all its emphasis on their security, frankly recognizes their weakness. The very essence of mind is to be weak — to be, at any moment, a mere present experience, more or less at war within itself and with its environment; yet also to be secure, for it can grasp ideals that give order to its experiences and beauty and control to its life. Nature, as we experience it, also is weak — a few fleeting sensations of the moment are all that we actually possess of it; yet it is secure, revealed by ideals to be a system of law. The weakness of ideals is like the weakness of mind and of nature; the security of ideals is the very source of the security of mind and of nature.

We have perhaps spoken as though mind, nature, and ideals were somehow three separate realms or powers. But the most adequate idealism rises above the separation which is made in ordinary experience and sees the union of the three. A universe in which ideals are so fundamental is believed by such idealism to be a universe of mind, a society of selves. My mind, indeed, faces an environment which is not my mind; but that entire environment is other mind. The positivistic view of science in Chapter II taught us that nature as known by science is a realm of human experience, actual and ideally possible, although produced by an other-than-human source; idealism goes further and sees in the physical nature which we experience a series of communications from a mind which orders the whole universe, and which religion worships as God. His will is the source both of nature and of ideals, as well as of minds.

Yet idealism of this type recognizes the variety as well as the unity of the work of the universal mind. The unity is organic; yet the variety is a real plurality. Hence we may call our view an organic pluralism. Since the whole effect of our study of mind, nature, and ideals has been to emphasize the organic aspect of reality, something specific should be said about its pluralism.

Reality seems to be plural in at least two senses. Every mind is itself, as we have seen, and not another. Hence, no mind is a part of any other mind; and it is just as impossible to believe my mind to be literally in God's mind as to believe my mind to be in yours. Each mind is distinct from its environment, however much its environment may affect it. Human minds are not, then, parts of the supreme mind; we are minds of our own, willed into being by the supreme mind, yet not merged in it or wholly controlled by it. This mutual otherness of minds means that, while the universe may have a single purpose, it is not a single mind.

A second type of variety in the universe is suggested with some diffidence. Nature, we have found, is nothing more than actual or possible experience of minds. In man's experience, plainly, nature is a force in part hostile and opposed to ideals, a source of delay and struggle. There have been many who have believed that there is a dualism of some sort in the universe between the forces of good and the forces of evil. The personification of the forces of evil in a personal devil, however, raises more problems than it solves. We no longer ascribe diseases and insanity to demons; they are in the course of nature. Nature seems to have taken the place of the devil. And yet, idealism finds nature to be the will of God. Here my diffident suggestion enters. Granted that nature is the will of God in action, is it possible that the struggle which we find in ourselves between nature and ideals is in some way a consequence of a struggle within the divine nature? I do not mean that the supreme mind has any inclination to evil. I mean rather that there may be in the very being of the divine mind, an element of experience which delays him, and which needs to be shaped and conquered by ideals, just as our sense experience needs to

be shaped and conquered. This would account for the
slow processes of evolution and progress in the world and
at the same time would be consistent with the ideal perfection of the supreme mind, since that would consist in
meeting every moment of experience with perfect loyalty
to the ideal.[38]

But whether these suggestions turn out to be true in
every detail or not is relatively unimportant. The great
abiding truth is the fact that mind and nature, although
not now ideal, are embodiments of ideals and that through
ideals alone can experience be theoretically understood or
practically controlled.

CHAPTER IV

SOURCES OF THE AUTHORITY
OF IDEALS

In the preceding chapters we have developed the foundations of a philosophy of ideals. We have held that ideals are not only of practical use to man in his control of experience, but also of theoretical use in revealing to him the very structure of the universe.

But this view will be greeted by many as similar views in the past have been greeted — with a certain skepticism. After all, they will inquire, granted that ideals are useful, can it be said that they are really imperative? Are they authoritative? The word authority is very unpopular at present, and is readily open to misunderstanding. In the modern disillusioned world, how fares it with the authority of ideals, in the light (or darkness!) of the actual social order in which we live?

Scholarship is one form of practical idealism. The scholar has a highly specialized task. Like Browning's " Grammarian," he must give up many other possibilities of his nature if he is to become a real scholar. He must concentrate. He must not only cut himself off from distracting tasks; he must also sever himself in certain respects from society. But he should never forget that the walls of his laboratory and his library were built by society, and that his task, no matter how specialized, is a social task. He should remember Plato's vision of a state in which philosophers are kings — remember it not with a view to seizing political powers, but with a view to realizing his social responsibilities. The practical kingship of scholars is acknowledged in current speech by a word which is used to describe a scholar. He is, men say, an authority. But his authority is somewhat precarious.

Authority is a word both honored and despised, expressing power yet betraying weakness. Is there, indeed, any authority for the modern man? Some writers avow that the modern temper consists in the absence of all authority. Be that as it may, old authorities have decayed; new ones are striving for recognition. In the family and the state, in church and school, in business and in pleasure — in every field — there is uncertainty about questions of authority.

If we reflect on the meaning of authority and inquire into its sources, it is without pretense of being able to discover any final solution of the problem. For our present purpose let us take authority to mean the power which prescribes to human beings what they shall do or think; or, more simply, the power which human beings obey — for they often obey powers which are not sufficiently intelligent to prescribe anything! And we shall be asking ourselves, What is the authority of ideals?

Every student of sociology is familiar with Tarde's *Laws of Imitation*. Tarde, followed by Ross and many

others, regards social life as consisting largely of imitation. But, as he points out, there must be something to
imitate. Imitation, therefore, presupposes invention.
But all of us are imitators to a greater extent than suits
our pride to admit. Yet to some extent — usually less
than we suppose — we are all inventors. We all contrib-
ute something which others imitate. In other words, we
obey authorities and we are authorities at the same time.
What then is the source of the authority to which we give
obedience? What is that in us which others recognize and
follow? What is the secret power of the commanding
ideal?

I

With our eye on the social facts, we must see at once
that a chief source of authority for the vast majority of
the human race, savage or civilized, is tradition and custom. The fact that a belief is held or has long been held
by others is commonly regarded as sufficient reason for
accepting the belief. Even truer is it that the fact that a
thing is done — is the fashion or the custom — is regarded by most human beings as a good enough reason
for doing it. The medicine man is nothing in himself, for
he is only the vehicle of tradition. But tradition and custom, powerful as they are, manifestly contain within
themselves no principle which justifies them in asserting
final authority over men.

Sometimes tradition is a wholesome and conserving
power; sometimes it is an unmitigated evil. Tradition

often opposes science and social progress; yet science and social progress are themselves ideals passed down by tradition. We cannot completely escape from the traditions of the society in which we live. If we indulge in an hysterical and undiscriminating revolt against all tradition, we are in danger of pouring out the baby with the bath. Tradition, then, is an actual sort of authority; its goods should somehow be conserved; but in a wholesome society tradition is subject to a higher authority than itself. It is a subordinate, not a commanding ideal.

II

Among those who rebel against tradition, it is commonly said that human desires are the higher court, the mandates of which tradition must obey.[1] Where social convention or religious creed stands in the way of the free fulfilment of natural desires, convention and creed must go. The son of man is lord of the Sabbath. Human need bids us cut red tape, say farewell to Mrs. Grundy, and reshape our whole society nearer to the heart's desire. Away with every institution which cramps basic human impulses!

In this doctrine there is a declaration of human independence which stirs the blood of many lovers of freedom and progress. Some of the most thorough and thoughtful minds of the modern world are in sympathy with it. But before their authority impels us to forsake all authority save that of our desires, we should pause to consider what this view means. The doctrine is that human desires

should be realized, not thwarted; that the happy life and
the happy society are those which have what they want.
The motto is " Back to Nature! " The fulfilment of desires is the supreme good. The suppression of desires is
the supreme evil. Freud, the anti-Puritans, and the anti-
prohibitionists strike hands in solemn compact. The only
moral absolute left — and it is very absolute — is the
categorical imperative, " Thou shalt do whatever thou
desirest and nothing else." This is the Supreme Court of
the new age. To interfere with the fulfilment of any
desires is contempt of court.

But as soon as one begins to think about the ideals of
this simple new Magna Charta, so soon one discovers
complications. Human desires fluctuate and often conflict with one another. The realization of an intense desire to enjoy life today may conflict with the realization
of an equally intense desire to be physically fit tomorrow.
If I fulfil my desires, you are prevented from fulfilling
yours. As soon as these elementary facts are recognized,
so soon new principles are generated which exercise authority over desire — the principles of self-control and
social responsibility. Bertrand Russell, himself one of
the most brilliant advocates of the authority of desire,
has rightly said that " the man who pretends to live independently is a conscious or unconscious parasite," [2]
that is, he is deceiving himself.

Moreover it is not alone human nature with its social
environment which limits and prescribes what desires may
be fulfilled and what may not. A larger nature, as we

have seen, surrounds us, and sets barriers to our wishes.
It not merely sets barriers; it also is capable of arousing
new desires which would not spring up of themselves unless there were a stimulus external to existing desires. He
who has once seen the Sistine Madonna desires to see it
again because he knows what it is. Nature is full of objects of desire. Edward Davison has beautifully expressed this thought in " The Snare." [3]

> Far away and long ago
> This trouble at my heart began;
> Ere Eden perished like a flower,
> Or Eve had shed her tears an hour,
> Or Adam knew himself a man,
> In every leaf of every tree
> Beauty had set a snare for me.
>
> Far away and long ago
> Her loveliest song began to chime.
> Bright Hector fell, and at the stroke
> Ten thousand hearts like mine awoke
> In every age and every clime.
> She stood bestriding Time and Space
> Amid the stars, and lit the rose
> With scent and color, and she chose
> My country for a dwelling place,
> And set a snare in every tree
> Awaiting me, awaiting me!

To put it in prose: life is not made happy and good by
getting what we happen to want but by learning intelligently to want the objectively best things. " Learning
to want " is not so Spartan and impossible as it may

sound to the disciples of desire. This principle points to the inner harmony between the objective beauty and truth in the universe and the deepest nature of man. How could it be otherwise, if man is native to the universe? But there is no sane authority on the surface of the life of desire, in mere surface-effects. "Die Klarheit," says Fichte, "ist nur in der Tiefe zu finden." "Clarity is only to be found in the deep places." Desire must obey the laws of truth or destroy itself. Life is more than a childish having of our own way, an indulgence of our whims and passions.

T. D. A. Cockerell has applied this thought to the realm of the esthetic. "If the modernist in art," he says, "then claims that the idea of beauty changes, and is purely subjective, we reply that to us there is also an objective standard of beauty, expressed in the perfection of a type according to its form and function. It is this response to objective reality, this harmony with nature, which seems to us to be the test of sanity." [4] To this may be added the apt remark of H. S. Canby, to the effect that "a standard of excellence in literature implies a criterion of beauty, a principle of ethics, an attitude in philosophy, and there can be no final judgment without due consideration of these fundamentals." [5] Desire cannot escape from the ideal of an authority higher than desire.

What, then, shall be said of desire as an authority? Actual authority it is. Desire commands and men obey. If they obey without rational controls and inhibitions, they do it to their ruin. They are self-deceived. Think-

ing that they are escaping from dependence on tradition
to a realm of real independence, they are only substitut-
ing for conscious imitation of their human fellows the
unconscious imitation of their animal ancestors. Instead
of making society their authority, they surrender themselves to certain aspects of their biological heredity. To
make desire a final authority is to invite chaos in the
inner life of the individual and the suicide of society. It
is a self-refuting ideal.

The cult of desire is sometimes thought to be realistic.
But the word " reality " is ambiguous. As M. R. Cohen
has said, too often " the praise of reality is the praise of
vivid sensations or emotions regardless of fitness or coherence." [6] A sane realism must carry us beyond the
immediate sensation and desire to the truth which they
imply and the ideal which they must obey.

All this does not mean that desire should be merely
suppressed or ascetically denied. It means rather that
desires should be developed and trained to fulfil their best
possibilities, as ivy is helped by the gardener to climb.
The sound principle has been in use among teachers and
students at the Barnes Foundation, where only those who
show interest are allowed to remain, and where interest is
defined as " an anxiety concerning future consequences
which impels the individual to do something to obtain
better consequences and avoid worse ones." [7]

III

Were we to follow out the strictly logical implications
of our study of desire as a source of authority, we should

be led to consider at once the authority of reason. But, since our aim is to keep close to the actual social facts, we must let logic wait for a time while we think of a different authority more potent than reason itself — a power which prescribes to millions of human beings what they shall do and think, and which they unhesitatingly obey. I mean the power of wealth. Wealth is a power which is both feared and loved.

The authority of wealth is too vast a subject for us to undertake a thorough discussion of it in this connection. Yet I cannot forbear touching on one point of vital interest to the scholar, namely, the authority of wealth in educational institutions. Wealth is necessary to a modern college. The individual Professor Vergil cannot expect a Mæcenas for himself; but the college as an institution requires wealthy patrons. Phi Beta Kappa itself seeks an endowment. Moreover, endowment funds, if they are to attain their end, must be invested in profit-yielding enterprises. Now, it is possible to picture a college endowed by wealthy friends whose methods of acquiring their wealth commend themselves neither to the department of Bible nor to that of ethics nor to that of economics or sociology.

If the liberal giver be also liberal-minded, and leaves the college free to use its best judgment in the expenditure of the gift, it is well. But what if a giver should expect a return in the form of perpetual support of his opinions by the college?

The necessary dependence of the college on wealth is partly heartening, partly ominous. It is heartening because many generous givers have rallied around worthy colleges, sharing the ideals of the college and glad to support it freely in the free devotion to truth. But it is ominous because of the possibilities of ill which lurk in the situation. Would it not be tragic if a twentieth-century Emerson should have to write of any American college or of anyone connected with American education as the nineteenth-century Emerson wrote of a great statesman?

> Why did all manly gifts in Webster fail?
> He wrote on Nature's grandest brow, *For sale.*

This awful peril can be averted, I believe, if the college plays its part. Men of wealth are not monsters. They are human beings, amenable to reason and to ideals. The function of the college is not to become the breeding place of fear or hatred of men of wealth, but rather to become a center which will enlighten rich and poor alike regarding the true values and ideals of life, and which will attract wealth to the service of ideals rather than debase ideals to the service of wealth. That our colleges have elicited the generosity and unselfish devotion of many men of means is one of the most encouraging features of American civilization; but it would be idle optimism to suppose that there is no danger from this source. The college is the brain, and, with the church, the conscience of society. The college, then, should admonish wealth to use its authority in the interests of a higher authority than wealth alone can confer.

IV

It is the consensus of enlightened opinion that traditions, desires, and wealth must, within certain limits, sub-
mit to the authority of law.

Law is the body of regulations which a society, or its
representatives, may impose for protection against the
antisocial conduct of its members or for the more effective
expression of social conduct.   No fair-minded person can
contemplate civilized society, despite its excesses and
abuses, without profound reverence for the majesty of the
law, which is, on the whole, save for certain glaring ex-
ceptions, voluntarily respected and obeyed wherever civilization extends.   If society is to survive, it is essential
that the authority of the law be maintained.   That it is
universally maintained is, of course, not true.   Too often
both the letter and the spirit of the law are flouted by the
modern man.

It, however, betrays a lack of perspective to attribute
all or most of current lawlessness to the attempt to en-
force the Eighteenth Amendment of the National Constitution.   The general restiveness of the age, the power of
wealth, the widespread demoralization consequent on war,
the indifference to moral and religious obligations, together with certain defects of the legal system — the law's
delays and its complicated technicalities — all tend to
weaken the authority of law throughout the world today,
even where there is no Eighteenth Amendment.   Incipient
lawlessness among good citizens is no local phenomenon,

easily remedied by freer access to alcohol. It is a symptom of a social disease, now acute but bidding fair to become chronic. The good citizen will be deeply concerned to understand and cherish the sources which give to law its authority and make it a binding ideal.

The reflective mind will indeed perceive that the law, although it embodies the sovereign power of the state, is not to be regarded as the ultimate source of all authority, much less as the sole authority binding on man. This is evident when one considers, for example, the process of the making and revision of law. The legislative power can command a law to be or not to be; or can change any existing law. The authority of that power is higher than that of any particular law which it makes. The legislators themselves must be elected by the people. Legislators and electorate! He who considers them as they are with the eye of a realist free from illusions cannot believe that either the average lawmaker or the average voter is an ultimate authority. Each is capable of indefinite improvement. Each should learn from a higher authority.

V

Who, then, can instruct the lawgiver and the voter? Now, as never before, one man claims that privilege as his right. That man is the scientist. The dullest mind of the twentieth century cannot fail to perceive the achievements and the prestige of science. Science has banished witches and demons from the life of the common man, and has brought him new health, power, and joy. Not only has science vast practical achievements to its credit; it has also revolutionized our view of life and of the world in many far-reaching ways. It has taken authority to sit in judgment on other pretended authorities.[8]

Science judges tradition. It sifts historical sources and subjects them, be they sacred or secular, to every test of textual, literary, and historical criticism. It is dominated by an objective interest in the facts and their explanation. It asks, What are the data? What causal laws can be discovered in the data? Science reverences truth, but it reverences no tradition which maintains as true what is shown by scientific investigation not to be true.

Science also judges desire. It has no interest in the question, How much do you like or dislike alcohol or restrictions on your personal liberty? It has great interest in such questions as, What are the actual effects on society of the use of alcohol or of certain restrictions on personal liberty? It is true that science can be used by the worst men for satisfying the worst desires. Chemistry may be applied by dietitians or by murderers. But even the most abandoned poisoner, if he is to succeed, must know the laws of the chemistry which he is applying. His desires have no effect on those laws. Science, then, is an authority which all desire must obey.

So too must wealth obey science. Science has no interest in what the rich man calls his " interests." But science has great interest in the economic, psychological, and social consequences of wealth and its accumulation, its use and its abuse.

Law, too, should obey the authority of science. Science — based on observed facts and their relations — gives light on the causes and cure of crime, the treatment of criminals, the public health, the conditions of public welfare. Contrast the old days when smallpox used to rage with these days of almost perfect immunity consequent on vaccination! Science commands the abolition of common drinking cups, and even those whose duty it is to administer the Holy Sacrament obey the authority of science. Legislation for the control of the rebellious Mississippi tarries until science discovers how to prevent floods. When science speaks clearly, law and wealth alike will obey.

Science is then our source of authority for matters of fact, save for those who still believe in magic. Science consists of verified laws of cause and effect. The majesty of science rivals the majesty of the law. Law is man-made; but science is made by observing nature itself. Law usually embodies the desires of society; science is objective and superior to all desires except the desire for truth. No right-thinking person will deny that science is an authority. The question with which the modern mind is struggling is not, Shall we cast off the authority of science? — but rather, Is there any other authority? Is the ideal of science the supreme ideal?

Is science the sole authority, the only power which a sane mind should obey? Many writers, with a wide popular hearing, are giving an affirmative answer to this question. A well-known house publishes a " Religion of

Science Library." Many are indeed giving to science the devotion which our forefathers once gave to religion alone. The nineteenth and twentieth centuries are the age of the great development and expansion of science. Is science to be the modern form, and the only form, of the knowledge of the glory of the Lord with which, according to the ancient seer, the earth will be filled? Is science, we ask again, the only authority?

An unqualified affirmative answer to this question, whether coming from the common man overawed by the material progress due to science or from the scientific worker himself with solid ground for confidence in experimental methods, rests, I am persuaded, on a confusion about the function and the field of science. Science, it is true, describes every observable fact and item of human experience. But all of the questions which science asks of experience are really forms of one question: What are the experienced facts, their causes, and their effects? Science, then, is interested in experienced events and the order which " explains " them. Natural science has no other problem.

Stated negatively, this is as much as to say what was said in Chapters II and III, namely, that natural science gives no direct light whatever on human obligations, human values, or human ideals. It sheds much indirect light on these realms, it is true. It describes our very experiences of value, individual and social. It tells what ideals can and what ideals cannot be realized, man and his environment being what they are. Granted that man

has an ideal which beckons him on, science will tell him
how best to attain that ideal. It describes fully all economic values — that is, instrumental values of exchange.
But, in the conflict of ideals, no mere description of facts
and their consequences will give us any ideal for the true
end of human living. Science does not tell us what human
beings ought to become, what values they ought to prize
as intrinsic, and what apparent values they ought to surrender. Science tells us what to do if we wish to live and
what to do if we wish to die; but science does not tell us
whether we ought to wish life or death for ourselves, and
much less does it tell us what the good life or the noble
death may be. Science is authority about the means of
life; it sheds no light on the ends.

It is true that all science involves intrinsic value in one
sense, but in one sense only. Science is possible only because men of science are devoted to the scientific ideal
and are convinced that there is value in its progressive
realization. Without moral idealism, science is impossible. This idealism captures the imagination in the cases
of men like Lister and Pasteur, whose life-work has bene-
fited the entire race. Less obvious, but no less idealistic,
is the romance in the work of a great theoretical physicist
like Lorentz, whose ideal of truth set him, as Bridgman
has recently said, the program of " extending the field
equations to small dimensions and following out the consequences. . . . That Lorentz saw," Bridgman goes on
to say, " that such a program might be carried through
must be recognized as a vision of extraordinary genius,

and that he was willing to devote to it the years of arduous and detailed calculation that he did is evidence of a pertinacity of purpose of the highest moral order." [9]   But Lorentz could not justify his idealism nor Bridgman his tribute by any experiments or laws within the field of physics.   Science does not prove ideals; it presupposes them.   Ideals make science possible as a human undertaking.   But the authority of ideals lies beyond the domain of natural science.

The facts which we have been considering confirm this conclusion: perfect scientific description sheds no direct light on what man ought to do.   It sheds light only on what he can do provided he accepts ideals which are not capable of being evaluated by scientific methods.   This conclusion men of science are often reluctant to accept. Yet it states the very essence of one aspect of scientific method.   Science must restrict itself to propositions about what is, has been, and will be; it contains no propositions about what ought to be.   Science speaks always conditionally: if certain conditions are fulfilled, certain consequences will follow.   It never speaks imperatively, saying, " Thou shalt seek the good, the beautiful, the holy, or the true."   Even the valuation of truth, as we have seen, is not a discovery, but a presupposition of science.   And if strictly scientific description is therefore incomplete and in need of supplementation, it is a necessary corollary that strictly scientific education is incomplete and in need of supplementation.

These statements are in no way to be construed as an

attack on science. To attack science would be as futile as to defend it would be superfluous. Moreover, the fact that the scientific spirit rests on and needs to be supplemented by moral values is cheerfully recognized by many of the most thoughtful scientists. Some writers, however, affect to regard this standpoint as a cowardly surrender of the truly modern scientific spirit to traditional Puritanism. It is to be noted, however, that these writers usually substitute for the spiritual ideal of the Roundhead the fleshly ideal of the Cavalier, as though, in some mysterious way, the latter were more scientific and modern. Moreover, such writers are more often dilettants than either scientists or philosophers. No; it is not from the authority of science that contemporary impuritanism springs, but from the sole authority of desire. Neither scientific — nor startlingly modern — is it to take as the moral ideal, " I want what I want when I want it."

If then the distinction between science and idealism is a sound one, it is worthy of most careful scrutiny, for our civilization more and more is taking science as its guide. The distinction grows out of, or is an aspect of, the fact discussed in a previous chapter, that science is abstract. For the purposes of any science, the facts are described from the point of view of that science only; everything else is treated as irrelevant. Practical difficulties in the treatment of disease sometimes arise for the poor man from the excessive abstraction of the science of medicine. Various abstractionists, called specialists, must in some instances be consulted before a case is either diagnosed or treated. Nevertheless, nothing is less intelligent than to regard abstraction with contempt. The department of mathematics in Boston University does well to take as its motto the saying of Michael Faraday, that " there is nothing so prolific in utilities as abstractions." Not abstraction, but fallacious inference from the fact of abstraction, is the parent of confusion.

Not only is each science and branch of science abstract relative to other sciences and branches, but science as a whole is abstract relative to the values of life. Science, as we have seen, abstracts from all ideals and values except the value of scientific description. If a scientific experimenter is to succeed in an experiment, he must concentrate on that experiment, forgetting everything else; and when a scientific law is formulated, it must be stated in the most abstract terms. The laws of physics, for instance, speak of movement without friction in a vacuum. The physicist must abstract from the fact that such conditions do not obtain in nature; and, in his capacity as theoretical physicist, he must also forget that experience reveals moral ideals (except in so far as physics itself depends on the moral will of a Lorentz).

It is becoming evident that, while nothing can supplant the authority of science within its own field, it is equally true that science itself cannot supplant the authority of ideals. Science is no absolute monarch, but rules under a constitution. Experience contains ideals and values as well as sense-data. Science treats ideals and values only as objects or processes to be described; it does not evaluate them. Nevertheless, we are not justified in turning from science to " ideals and values," and finding in that formula the source of authority, for we are concerned in looking for the source of the authority of ideals and values themselves. If ideals are to be our guide, we must ask, What ideals? Whose ideals? Why? The " Conflict of Ideals " is the death knell of all sentimental and uncritical idealism. Is there any power which can survey clashing value-claims, can investigate the many pretenders to the throne of authority in human life, and assign to each its place?

Some will reply that there is no such power, because there is no possible answer to the question. There is, they think, no fixed place to which values can be assigned. Ideals are changing, relative, unstable. And these objections are partly sound. New times, new manners. Babbitt is an ideal which, for good or ill, would have been impossible fifty years ago and will be impossible fifty years from now. Deeper ideals of morality and religion change their face with startling rapidity. Are we back in the chaos of desire? Are ideals only the *mores* of the moment? Is value valuable only because it happens to be socially approved? Is fashion or expediency, then, the court of last resort?

These problems are not lightly to be set aside. But neither is human nature and experience itself lightly to be set aside. And the same human nature which contains the chaos of desires and the warfare of conflicting standards also contains the function for their control, namely, the reason. The reason is none too popular today; but before we yield to the clamor of those who believe that there is some way of finding truth above or beyond or, at any rate, other than, reason, we should consider carefully reason's claim to be the ultimate source of authority.

VI

By reason is meant that function of the mind which views the objects of experience in their connection, coherently and synoptically. Reason is not satisfied to leave any fact in isolation; it demands connection, relation, system. It seeks reality in its togetherness. It is evident that science, which we have just been considering, is a typical product of reason. The syllogism, with its laws of necessary inference, is another aspect of reason. But the scope and nature of reason are but feebly grasped by one who regards reason as confined to science and the syllogism. Consider the act of the mind in composing or rendering or appreciating a great work of music, let us say Handel's " Largo." Who can listen to those stately and mystical measures without perceiving a unitary system of experience, a coherently beautiful interpretation, which is no less interpretation because it is not science and no less reason because it is not syllogism? Every work of art is a work of reason, a harmonious and meaningful creation of mind. A poem or a statue without meaning or coherence is both inartistic and irrational. Beauty is not made by mere expression of whatever is in one; the expression must be of something which is worthy, that is, rational. Likewise, love and religion are true love and true religion only when they are experiences of genuine inner harmony, unity, meaning. They too are forms of reason. Life, we are told, is more than logic; but let us remember that reason is itself more than formal logic. Reason is harmony, unity, order, wholeness, wherever it expresses itself, and through whatever medium. Unreason is discord, contradiction, incoherence, disharmony.

The ideal of reason is one with the ideal of philosophy. To make philosophy the guide of life is to make reason the guide of life. Indeed, it may be said that the true function of education, as distinguished from mere training — and, in particular, the function of the college of liberal arts — is the cultivation of reasonableness in as many fields as possible. Heretical though it may be, I stand with Alexander Meiklejohn in the belief that the justification for the existence of the college is that it fulfils an intellectual function.[10] If the person who goes to college aims chiefly at learning how to make money, he should go directly into business; if he aims chiefly at athletics, almost every town has a bowling alley and a local gymnasium; if he yearns solely for social life, why be distracted by studies? — and even if he seeks character as his exclusive interest, it is difficult to see why his local Sunday School might not help him in that direction without his engaging in the irrelevancies of the life of a student. The college teaches, or should teach, understanding of the present and the past, not alone for the practical purpose of control of the future (although rational control of the future is most important), but also for the cultural purpose of furnishing sources of delight for man's leisure hours, when he may, if you please, loaf and invite his soul, his soul being rational.

Is this defense of reason merely academic? No; there are few problems more practical than those connected with a truly rational use of leisure time. Without a solution of this problem, neither the labor problem nor any distressing social problem, will ever be solved. And no problem is settled rightly until it is settled rationally, that is, in the light of all the facts, and consistently with the demands of the whole situation. When the cultivation of living reason among students in colleges is seen to be no mere imposition of professorial taskmasters, nor yet the indulgence of the selfish tastes of gifted scholars, but rather the essential health and progress of society, then both the cultural and the practical functions of the colleges will be better fulfilled and we shall be on the way to a new civilization. Then students will see, for example, that there are no dead languages, but only dead minds; that no science or history is uninteresting, but that interest is killed by the inattention of a slumbering reason; and that life is not in any way rendered happier or better by being lived unreasonably.

Yet, as I have already intimated, the place of reason as a source of authority is called in question by many. Certain " special interests " are, or — letting their cat out of the bag — think they are, imperiled by rational investigation. Hence, on the lips of some the words " reason " and " rationalism " become synonymous with skepticism about life's highest values. This conception of reason is a patent misconception. Reason is not essentially an instrument of denial but an instrument of vision. What appears false to the best reason must be false so far as the human mind can judge. It is little less than tragic — although in some cases it can only be called cheap — when friends of morality and reason see in religion a foe. Reason and religion stand or fall together. As John Locke has said, " He that takes away reason to make way for revelation, puts out the light of both." [11] Religion rests on the faith that the universe is reasonable.

Others try to put reason in bad repute by means of the psychology of rationalization, which shows us that human nature is apt at thinking up reasons to justify us in seeking the fulfilment of our desires. The tendency to rationalization is said by some psychologists and philosophers to be the real ground for the historic systems of philosophy. We desire the universe to be good, true, and beautiful. Idealism is the rationalization of that desire.[12] Thus an attempt is made to discredit the achievements of reason. And yet, if reason can be discredited thus, it must follow that psychology itself and every scientific process which appeals to reason is also discredited. Unless reason, in the broad sense in which we are using the term, be truly authoritative, there is literally no reason for any authority or for any conduct.

Even some representatives of rational systems, such as law and science, manifest a certain failure to appreciate reason.   In the case of law, the conflict is perhaps less intelligible.   Law is essentially social; reason, while it is social by virtue of being universal and common to all, is individual in the sense that each man must think for himself, as no man in society can legislate for himself.   Thus, from the point of view of law, reason is a principle of anarchy.   It may be urged that the anarchistic use of reason is an abuse; true, but who will guarantee the correct use of reason by human beings?   A real conflict will probably always exist here until all legislation is rational and all rational beings arrive at perfection.

The conflict between science and reason arises from " the cult of science " — the tendency to regard all use of reason beyond the limits of science as spurious.   An article by W. M. Davis well expresses this point of view.[13] There is no knowledge, he thinks, save what is experimentally verifiable, that is, science.   Applying this veto to ethics, he expresses the hope that " ethics may be redeemed by making it an inductive and therefore truly scientific study of the natural history of goodness."   Now, there are two fundamental objections to this reduction of the authority of reason to the description of phenomena. The first is that a complete natural history of goodness would tell us only what has been and is thought good, but would tell us nothing about what ought to be thought good or what we ought to do; Davis's ethics would be only data for ethics, but would not contain a single ethical proposition.   The second objection is that the demand for verifiable knowledge alone rests on an inadequate idea of verification. Davis desires a verifiable natural history of goodness; yet, strictly speaking, no genuinely past event can be verified. Moreover, all verification is relative to the knowledge and beliefs of the verifying person. No experiment can occur without a guiding and interpreting mind. All verification, then, and all science fall within the larger domain of the total system of reason.

Again, there are those who would free human life from the restraints of reason by the curious device of dividing theory sharply from practice and holding that reason dwells in the former but not in the latter realm. These persons tell us that the pursuit of truth should be carried on quite irrespective of its practical consequences, even of its moral consequences. We agree heartily with them in holding that truth should be obeyed, however painful obedience may be. But it is impossible to understand by what right reason is supposed to disregard consequences. A rational mind will abhor irrational consequences; and a rational mind will be under bonds to treat practical consequences as rationally as it treats abstruse theory. One need not be a sectarian pragmatist to hold that irrational practice is probably symptomatic of irrational theory. Moreover, free and brave truth-seeking must be *truth*-seeking. Without an allegiance to the ideal of truth like that of Lorentz, no reasoning can be carried through. Logic, the Germans rightly say, is " die Moral des Denkens," " the ethics of thinking." Furthermore, truth includes truth about consequences. Truth-seeking cannot then be wholly indifferent to moral consequences without destroying its own foundations. The truth-seeker must be loyal to rational ideals and must seek the whole truth about all ideals.

All attempts, therefore, to cast off the authority of reason eventuate in failure. Science, morality, religion, civilization itself must be reasonable or must be untrue to their own inner nature and implications. Reason is then a source of authority which all other authorities should consult and obey. Reason does not create the game of life, but it is the umpire of every play. It is the ideal of ideals. The results of Chapter III are thus confirmed by our social approach.

VII

Are we now at the end of our search? Is reason the supreme source of authority? It might well seem that an affirmative answer is the only possible one. What can be truer, fairer, more worthy of obedience, than the highest reason? Are not the facile attacks on reason, launched against it by popular sophists, an appeal for us to abandon the true, the good, and the beautiful for what is easier of attainment than they? — to leave the lofty for the low? And is this appeal convincing when made in the name of the flesh, or should it be more so when made — as it too often is — in the name of the Lord?

Yet, if we use our reason properly, we shall perceive that there is danger of committing at this point what Bowne called the fallacy of the universal. Reason, we are saying, is authority. But what reason? Or more accurately, whose reason?

The truth seems to be that reason as an abstraction has no more existence or authority than, say, " the state." No one is loyal to " the state " in general; millions are loyal to the United States of America and to France. Reason in general commands nothing; Aristotle's reason challenges every mind that is a mind. Abstract reason, then, cannot be the final source of authority, simply because there is no such reality as mere reason. There are only particular persons who, more or less successfully, embody reason. Indeed, apart from persons, apart from the incarnation of the "Logos," no authority of any sort has force or exists. It is clear enough that tradition, desire, science, and law are but ways in which persons feel, think, or act. Wealth, as physical fact, does not intimidate or inspire, but wealthy persons and groups of persons are authorities. No authority, apart from a person who obeys or acknowledges it, has any being or potency.

Personality, then, is the final seat of authority, the source of all sources. The ultimate ideal is " for, of, or in a person." [14] I and we should find our authority in human nature, individual and social; or more accurately, in the nature of persons, for society has no existence apart from the attitudes and behavior of the individuals composing it.

This principle, which I believe to be true, is like most truths dangerous. It lends itself to mistreatment; for personality may be a spurious form of authority. Personal charm or force of will or impulse may lead men to the worst of conduct. This fact is, of course, proof that personality is an actual authority, but at the cost of raising doubt about its ideal authority. Further, every false and misleading authority is, in some sense, personal.

He who interprets the value of personality should, then, be cautious and explicit in his thought. Personality is no authority because I am I and you are you; much less because I am a super-I and stronger than slave-you.[15] Though it be true that reason is nothing apart from personality, it is also true in the long run that personality is nothing worth having apart from reason — if by reason we mean the spirit of inner unity and meaning, and not merely the formal technique of the schools. The Latin proverb applies: " ratio et consilium propriae ducis artes." Reason and deliberation are the proper qualities of the leader, and, we may add, of every true person. The authoritative person is then the person who aims at the rational control of all his powers in the light of his highest, that is, his most rational, ideals. This sort of person will work with and learn from others in so far as they too are seeking control through ideals. The rational person sees himself as member of a social community and of a cosmos. The men who are trusted as authorities are men on whom we rely as being loyal to ideals. We may err in our confidence in a maker of tradition, or a controller of desire, or a builder of science, or a creator of wealth, or a lawmaker, or a reasoner; but when we justly repose confidence in him, it is because we see in him one whom we believe to be rationally loyal to his ideal.

If we are challenged by one who asks, Why, then, so much ado about personality? — we reply by an appeal to reason. Reason exists only in persons, and it exists for the development of persons, for their orientation in the world of nature and society and in the inner world of individuality. Reasonable personality is the end; reason the means. Above all, we add, personality is the supreme authority because reason itself is impotent or even dangerous without love. Without a love of truth — of some truth, at least — reason will not be exercised; and without a love of man the love of truth either is not awakened or being awakened is sterile. Not Jesus of Nazareth only, but Confucius, Buddha, Plato, Aristotle, and Spinoza, with many others, have seen in love — that is, in the desire for the sharing of perfection among persons — the consummation of personality and the source of infinite growth.

If we accept reasonable, loving personality, loyal to the ideal of a shared perfection of all persons, as the true source of all individual and social authority, we have reached a central spiritual principle on which civilization rests. The aim of this chapter is not merely to point to this familiar truth, but also to show how all the authority of all ideals depends on the appeal to this one.

At the outset of the chapter it was said that the scholar is commonly called an authority. The true scholar is indeed an embodiment of the principle at which we have arrived. His authority is no external force, no mere compulsion of others. It is an appeal to rational control. To the frantic freedom of an unrestrained expression of every random impulse this authority opposes a view of human nature as a whole. The youth of today affirms the abstract principle of personality: I am my own authority. The college often affirms the abstract principle of reason: truth is the authority. Neither principle is adequate when taken alone; both are true when taken together. I am my own authority only when I have committed myself to the love of truth, that is, to the love of persons as they ought to be. The problem of authority, then, is the problem of developing persons who, in the full sense of both words, love to be true.

CHAPTER V

MERE IDEALISM

In Chapter IV consideration was given to some of the fundamental questions about the roots of ideals. But the point of view developed in Chapters I, II, and III is subject to attack from another quarter. Most thoughtful minds will grant that, in some sense, ideals are authoritative, however changing and subject to revision they may be. But many object to having this truth labeled as "idealism," even when the word does not denote any special metaphysical system. Their objection becomes much livelier when idealism is taken to mean what in the last analysis most "idealists" take it to mean, namely, that the real universe is a system of communicating selves. This view, contemptuously called mentalism,[1] is the pet aversion of many recent thinkers.

It has not always been thus and, I venture to predict, will not always be. Idealism has had a checkered history which reflects changing moods in civilization. In early nineteenth-century Germany or in the America of Emerson and the Concord School, to call a man an idealist was to praise him as a man of reason and sense. In the Germany or the America of today, the idealist is often regarded as the impractical dreamer, the man whose head is in the clouds and whose feet consequently are not on the ground. During the war we were all idealists; or, to be more accurate, we all paid lip-service to idealism. Since the war, as Lord Birkenhead has said frankly at Williamstown, the policy is national self-interest; [2] or, as a prominent editor has told college students, we want none of this " cant about humanity." In this social atmosphere one who ventures to peep and mutter against contemporary tendencies in order to say a few kind words for idealism may well do so humbly. He must confess that his subject is mere idealism.

If it were only philosophical idealism of which we were thinking, we might take refuge in the blessed thought that there is no distinction in being in the minority. Very rarely has it been true that any type of philosophical system could claim the adherence of a majority of living philosophers. Every opinion is a minority opinion. Yet, while this is true, it is doubtless also true that idealism is in a smaller minority today than it was in the year 1904. In that year, a clear majority of the speakers at the Philosophical Division of the Congress of Arts and Sciences at St. Louis were avowed idealists of one sort or another; and they were all representative philosophers.[3] A similar showing could hardly be made today. Realism, pragmatism, and naturalism are now much stronger than they were twenty years ago. Most of the great philosophers who have died in recent years were idealists: Bradley, Bosanquet, Ward, Rashdall, M'Taggart in England; Bowne, Royce, Münsterberg, and Creighton in the United

States. The men who are filling their places are such men as Russell, Broad, Moore in England, and Montague, Dewey, Perry in this country, with Whitehead recently come from England to America, all realists of one sort or another. I do not mean that there are no conspicuous idealists left; I mean only that the ranks are thinned.

For the purposes of this chapter, at least, we shall understand idealism to mean the belief that the visible present reality ought to be interpreted in accordance with some ideal which is not visibly present. You might almost say that idealism interprets the present by means of the absent, while realism interprets the absent by means of the present. The latter procedure on the face of it seems much more sensible. But the idealist obstinately asserts that the present and visible real derives its meaning from the absent and invisible ideal.

This does not get us far, however, for we are still in the dark about the word ideal. The typical unphilosophical realist will tell you that the ideal is a dream, an unreality, or at best a state of affairs that is desired but does not exist. To some extent this is true; but it overlooks the difference between random desires and true ideals, that is, between surface-effect and depth-effect. A true ideal is a conceptual scheme of some kind which the mind acknowledges to be binding on its procedure.[4] Not all desired objects are ideals; nor are all images of the absent. True ideals are imperative principles which we see that we ought to abide by. The principles of logic and of

scientific method we have found to be good illustrations
of ideals, as is also moral obligation.

Now the idealist insists that persons and things, nations
and property, scientific experiments and wars become
significant only through their relation to ideals. They
are to be estimated through the ideals which they tend to
realize. Hoernlé has recently remarked that " idealism,
as Josiah Royce once said, is ' the expression of the very
soul of our civilization.' It will prove a vain fancy only
if our civilization has no soul to express." [5] That is, if
ideals are not true, nothing is. Yet it is also true that a
mere ideal, which is not realized or expressed as far as
possible, is utterly valueless. We have already found
that only an ideal realized in actual experience, or in
process of realization, is of value.

I

As one hears the issue stated, one vacillates between
the feeling that every sensible man and no sensible man
is an idealist, as the term has been defined.

Be that as it may, the woods are full of conscientious
objectors to idealism. The practical man, the natural
scientist, the psychologist, and the philosopher all have
their suspicions, which all are willing to voice. Nevertheless, the aim of this chapter is to show that all who are
opposed to idealism are at heart idealists who do not quite
understand themselves or the idealism which they reject.
It may be that the lower animals do not live by ideals, although it is permitted to doubt even that; but to be

human, as I shall try to show, is to idealize. This point
may be illustrated at the outset from two or three thinkers
who reject metaphysical idealism. Among others, E. G.
Spaulding, the neo-realist, has demanded " a neo-realism
of ideals " ; [6] and M. C. Otto, the pragmatist, in his book
suggestively entitled *Things and Ideals,* says, " Those
who scoff at the idealists are of the same genus but of
another species." [7]

II

The practical man has always been impatient with the
person who set himself to follow the gleam. It was, you
may be sure, an idealist who proposed in the eighteenth
century to found a college in Bermuda to teach the In-
dians the Hebrew language and the principles of Christianity; the same man, good Bishop Berkeley, as he is
patronizingly called, also being the author of the *Siris,*
that amazing work which praises idealism and the virtues
of tar-water to heal all human ills. It may be remarked
parenthetically that it was not his philosophy (which was,
in my opinion, on the whole true) but his tar-water
(which was ridiculous) that won the idealist a hearing
among the practical men of his day. They were willing
to tolerate his idealism for the sake of his magic medicine.
And yet the idealism was, in the best sense, more practical
than the tar-water.

The objections of the practical man are not wholly
based on the virtues of tar-water. He finds what he regards as substantial grounds for impatience with the
idealist. Ideals, he holds, take our mind away from pres-

ent facts which must be reckoned with; lead to fantastic
schemes; cause men to waste time on foolish inventions
and theories. C. D. Broad, himself a philosopher, has
recently spoken of " silly " philosophies — "which may
be held at the time when one is talking or writing pro-
fessionally, but which only an inmate of a lunatic asylum
would think of carrying into daily life." Broad counts
behaviorism and certain forms of idealism as "silly" in
this sense and thinks that " only very acute and learned
men could have thought of anything so odd or defended
anything so preposterous against the continual protests
of common-sense." [8] A philosopher must be very hostile
to idealism when he bases his objection to it on that most
unphilosophical foundation, common sense. The practical man, however, is at once convinced by such an attack
as the one just quoted. Does not idealism often lead men
to ignore the physical needs of life in the pursuit of impractical theories? It may be well enough for a Socrates,
a Jesus, a St. Paul, or an Abraham Lincoln to chase ideals;
it is too risky for Mr. and Mrs. Practical Man and the
children. For them it is silly.

In this protest against an idealism which destroys or
ignores the physical basis of life, the practical man is not
wholly wrong. Surely some pretended ideals are silly.
They can never be realized and ought never to be. The
real meaning of the protest of the practical man is that
we should beware of false ideals. But he is not so clear
as to what should be substituted for false ideals. No
ideals? Or true ones? And what true ones?

Yet there is danger that the best and truest of ideals

will seem impractical to the impatient citizen who takes
as his own the Hebrew's version of the motto of the ancient Romans, S. P. Q. R., rendered, " Small Profits,
Quick Returns." Frank Roscoe has said, " There should
be a new litany for the middle-aged: ' From the loss of
our enthusiasms and from the perils of practical experience, good Lord deliver us.' " [9] The highest and most
necessary ideals must be realized gradually, and must be,
in the earlier stages of their realization, impractical. The
practical man resents mention of an ideal which cannot
be realized in time to be reported in the early edition of
the afternoon paper. This resentment arises in part from
his eager devotion to the ideal and his sense of the value
of time. But the practical man must learn how slowly
grind the mills of the gods. Any ideal, like any operation,
is for a while most uncomfortable; only in the long run
does the healing power of truth become evident. Even
the cranks and radicals, whom the practical man detests
and fears, are explorers and experimenters in the realm
of the ideal and in the long run may be justified. History
should instruct us.

What, then, has the practical man a right to say to the
mere idealist? He dare not say to the prophet, prophesy
not; nor to the idealist, cease idealizing. He dare not
measure ideals by their present results, especially not
by the results in economic production and " efficiency."
What he can say, and what at heart he is trying to say,
is this: " Show me, O idealist, that these ideals of which
you talk truly ought to be realized and show me how they

can be realized. Show me that they are not wholly weak
and fragile. It is easy enough, I admit, for a mere thinker
to talk about ideals; or for a mystic to feel them. Show
me that the strong man of action needs ideals." The
mood of the practical man is likely to be strengthened
when he reads in the public press statements like the following, " The United States has less material interest in
China than Great Britain, and hence can afford to be
more idealistic." [9]

The objection of the practical man, then, really reduces
to an earnest reassertion of the belief that unrealized
ideals are worthless and that idealists must have true
ideals which they faithfully seek to realize. At heart,
the practical man did not mean to say " mere idealism,"
but rather, " more idealism." B. M. Laing speaks for the
practical man when he says, " We may envisage an ideal
world in which only the desired and the desirable exist,
and we may picture people living in this world and seeking the good; but unless this world is brought into relation
with the real forces at work in human life, it will remain
' in the air. ' " [10]

III

A while ago I remarked that the natural scientist is
also to be counted among the objectors to idealism. This
assertion is to be taken with a grain of salt. There are
few members of the community more devoted to ideals
than are the men of science. Without integrity, industry,
trustworthiness, and loyalty to the ideals of truth and

scientific method there could be no science at all. Science
is the cooperative enterprise of honorable men with the
highest attainable standards in their field.

Nevertheless it remains true that some men of science
object to some ideals which the human race has long
cherished; and there arises an artificial barrier between
science and idealism, for which in fact there is no real
reason. If this book could help in breaking down that
barrier, it would be justified. When such scientists as I
have mentioned undertake to justify their critique of
ideals, they argue that ideals go beyond the facts; and
facts, they feel, are final. Particularly is this true, some
scientists believe, of religious ideals. Religious ideals are
speculative and doubtful, in their opinion; scientific ideals
are proved. Sometimes confidence in scientific ideals,
however, leads men of science to the rather amusing position of finding final truth in the present state of scientific
knowledge. Not long ago a distinguished scientist pub-
licly stated in my hearing that science is absolute; and
within ten minutes in the same lecture added that science
is pretty radically revised every thirty years. A new
absolute every thirty years is distinctly an American
ideal! Another scientist in his zeal for evolution (a most
worthy zeal in a most worthy cause) found himself saying over the radio [11] that the literalist view of the Bible
" is not only puerile, it is insulting, both to God and to
human intelligence. But the fundamentalist would do
much worse than insult God." The ' much worse ' is to
deny God's growing revelation; this denial is said to be

an " evil influence, criminal, damnable." In short, it is
" as blasphemous as it was for the Jewish leaders to say
of Jesus that ' He casts out devils through Beelzebub, the
prince of the devils.' " In other words, to deny evolution is asserted to be the sin against the Holy Spirit. One
cannot repress the feeling that a man who takes such a
position is lacking in perspective. Fundamentalism
doubtless needs criticism. But dogmatic assertion of the
finality of scientific knowledge is hardly the best way to
refute dogmatic assertion of the finality of religious
knowledge.

Now, the frame of mind which defends scientific ideals
and attacks others (even false ones) on the ground that
the present state of scientific knowledge is a realized
ideal, and the only ideal worthy of consideration, is really,
in practice, a good deal more common than we might like
to admit. When, for example, J. H. Leuba writes a book
on *Belief in God and Immortality,*[12] he tries to show that
the more distinguished men of science are, the more
likely they are to doubt the religious beliefs of mankind.
If this be true, I wonder whether it is because those men
of science have given the religious ideals the same careful
scrutiny they have given scientific ideals, or whether their
allegiance to the ideals of science has not narrowed their
interest and contracted their appreciation until they believe that scientific ideals are the only ideals worthy of
consideration. The ideals of science are indeed valid and
cover a vast range of human thought; woe be to the advocate of other ideals who ignores science! Yet after

all, in the empire of the ideal, science is but a province; in the constitution of the universe, provision for science is but one article, and that, perhaps, neither the first nor the last.

IV

There is a new science difficult to classify, the relation of which to idealism should be considered. Psychology in its modern forms is both so complex and so immature that it is asserted both to be and not to be a natural science; some regard it as a branch of physiology, others regard all sciences and philosophy as parts of psychology; and between these extremes lie many intermediate positions. Despite its confusions, which we discussed in Chapter I, psychology is bringing to our attention many facts which have been ignored or misunderstood in the past, and it has something to say about our problem of idealism.

Indeed, no doubts about ideals are more corroding, more utterly annihilating (if true) than those proposed by some modern psychologists. The net outcome of certain lines of psychological thought may be stated briefly as follows. Ideals are nothing but desires which have a biological or subconscious basis in the last analysis connected with sex. The real nature of an ideal is, as Freud would say, suppressed by the censor; but the psychologist can outwit the censor by psychoanalysis and discover that all ideals are rooted in certain unrealized sexual desires. A suppressed desire is an amazingly creative power; it builds dreams in sleep and waking hours, writes poems, carves marble, founds religions and philosophies, all of which mean only, " My sex life is maladjusted." A recent writer finds profound psychological significance in the fact that " Jehovah is Father, but the mother image is repressed." [13] For him, as for numerous others, God is " father-complex " and religion a mere series of symbols for our subconscious difficulties and adjustments.

For this psychoanalytic point of view (which, be it noted, is not shared in its extreme form by all psychoanalysts) religion is what is called a rationalization; *i. e.*, it is a system of imaginary ideas intended subconsciously as a compensation for real experiences which are lacking. If we accept this view (I almost said, this ideal), we shall have to say that all ideals are more or less disguised pictures of a world in which we could have our own way; the Mohammedan paradise of indulgence is psychologically frank, while the censor still operates in the Christian heaven of the hundred and forty and four thousand who are virgins.

Such a reading of the most sacred aspirations of humanity is revolting to the feelings. Yet one does not have to be a student of abnormal psychology to see that there is some truth in the principle for which the new psychology is pleading. The intelligent observer of everyday life will see for himself that man's desires influence his conduct. Man desires a certain type of physical stimulus; this desire enables him to work out an elaborate scheme of rationalization which justifies him in violating

the law and constitution of his country by about the same
sort of reasoning as the bandit uses, if he is so delicate as
to feel the need of reasoning. We decline to go to the
doctor lest we discover that we are more ill than we desire
to be. We want this world to end and another to be
initiated by the coming of Christ and believe accordingly.
We want property and comfort and believe, therefore,
that if capitalism were destroyed, we should have property and comfort. There is no doubt about the fact
that conscious or unconscious desires, often based on
biological tendencies, mold both our ideals and our
conduct, without regard to common sense, reality, or
possibility. There is nothing, it might almost be said,
so absurd but what it will be believed by a person who
desires it.

But when psychology goes to the extreme of interpreting the normal by the abnormal, it shows a lamentable
lack of perspective. If carried out to the end, this would
amount to saying that all ideals of all moralists, religion-
ists, philosophers, and scientists, save those of abnormal
psychologists, are false; while abnormal psychology alone
has the key to human life and understands thoughts and
motives as they truly are. When a person is so passionately loyal to one ideal as to deny all others, he is usually
called a faddist or a fanatic; he is sometimes said to be
the victim of an obsession. The abnormal psychologist
should be the first to see and to avoid the peril of obsession. Unfortunately, he is not always awake to his own
inconsistency.

If the psychoanalytic account of ideals were wholly

true, it would be very difficult to rescue psychological ideals from the general ruin. Some ideals are, indeed, rationalizations of desire, as we have seen; and the undiscriminating idealist who follows every pretended ideal with equal ardor has set himself an impossible and absurd task. But the very fact that we are able to judge some ideals to be impossible and absurd implies that we appeal to other ideals as sound. If we can judge one ideal to be a mere rationalization of desire, it is because we acknowledge another ideal as leading us to truth about the human mind. Further, it is not rational to assume that all reasoning which arises from desire is false or evil, even if the desire be sexual in character. Desire to win the war greatly stimulated the discovery of scientific truth, as R. W. Nelson has pointed out. The truth of an ideal, then, cannot be tested by the nature of the desire which occasioned its origin. Perhaps the first savage who learned to count did so in a desire to overreach a fellow tribesman in barter; yet if this were so, it would not prove that arithmetic is dishonest or is a mere rationalization of the desire to cheat. Perhaps Shelley's poetry was an outgrowth of his unhappy sex-life; but this is far from proving that his poems contain no ideal truth. On the contrary, it might well lead us to suspect that in the very instinct of sex there is a yearning for ideal truth, a yearning which may misunderstand itself and go astray but which may also lead the mind to visions of true beauty and goodness. But I can hear E. D. Martin saying, " Platonism is a perfect escape mechanism; " [14] and I freely admit that, if he is right in his view of ideals, I am wrong.

Psychology, then, has dealt searchingly with ideals. But it has no valid objection to all ideals. It vetoes sentimentalism, truly enough; demands critical scrutiny, and forthright rejection of ill-founded ideals. But it does so in the interests of the ideal of truth, and so of the truth of ideals. In the service of ideals, it warns us against being deceived by seeming ideals. It shows that ideals may have the form but lack the power of idealism. From the psychologist, the idealist must learn discipline, and must discover how to guard himself against being carried away by his own lusts and enticed when he thinks he is doing God service. But when the psychologist seems to say that we should reject all ideals because of the perils of the way, he is so cautious as to destroy the possibility of his own science.

V

Some educators, also, are uneasy about ideals. G. B. Watson, of Teachers College, lists five difficulties.[15] " (1) The proposed virtues, traits and ideals never exist as units. . . . (2) The direction of attention toward character traits, virtues and ideals reverses the conditions which make ethical living possible. . . . (3) Emphasis upon traits, virtues and ideals leads to an educational practice which neglects many of the fundamental causes of desirable and undesirable behavior. . . . (4) Character traits, virtues and ideals represent moral ruts, and as such tend to interfere with creative ethical living. . . .

(5) There are many important ethical problems with which training in traits, virtues and ideals intensifies the difficulty rather than aids in solution."

This rather alarming indictment, when examined critically, is seen to rest on the assumption that ideals are standardized and atomistically separate patterns of conduct. But if, as Watson hints, character is an organic, living unity and not " a summation of traits," [16] and if the ideal is a conception of the direction of growth of a free and creative life, the criticisms are seen to be directed, not against ideals, but against conventionalized and dead views of ideals.

A discussion by a contemporary German popular educator, Johannes Müller, rests on much the same assumptions and leads to much the same results.[17] But Müller attacks idealism more bitterly than Watson criticized ideals. Idealism, says Müller, is " a source of illusions," leading man to " a hypocritical self-righteousness " ; it " completely ignores the reality of things," and assumes that " everything is possible and attainable! " " The ideal is only a phantom." And yet, having said this, he pleads for the creative development of personality and for obedience to what God gives! Like every other critique of idealism, Müller's turns into a plea for idealism of a special kind. Both Watson and Müller are misled into drawing unwarranted theoretical conclusions from their practical problems as educators. Difficulty in realizing the ideal does not mean that idealism is false, but rather that it needs to be understood more thoroughly.

VI

We have found that most criticisms of idealism are made by idealists who fail to understand themselves. In some way, every criticism of mere idealism turns out to be an appeal to the authority of mere ideals. This at least has been found to be true of the criticisms of practical men, natural scientists, psychologists, and educators. But we have not probed to the root of the unrest about ideals until we have consulted the philosophers.

It is true that all philosophers will be stigmatized at the start by some as " mere idealists," no matter what school of philosophy they profess. The red-blooded practical man usually has no use for philosophy. The very word affects him somewhat as does the quadrisyllable Bolshevism — which means something evil, he knows not what. But red blood does not necessarily qualify one as a judge either of Bolshevism or of philosophy. President A. Lawrence Lowell of Harvard University has remarked that red blood is that which has not passed through the brain. Be that as it may, if anyone is to reject the wisdom of philosophy, he will find himself obliged to give himself and others a philosophic reason for doing so — and there he is, back within the fold of philosophy where men try to see life as a whole.

Yet, however philosophers may appear to the outsider, they do not seem to themselves to be all idealists. In one sense, indeed, they are; for almost every serious philosophical thinker has been earnestly devoted to the higher

ideals of life. All philosophers would agree that men
should devote themselves to truth, should interpret facts
by laws, and should acknowledge ideals as binding. But
despite this agreement there have always been quarrels
among philosophers about the meaning of ideals. One
party, as we have seen from the outset of this book, holds
that ideals are not only man's guide in the control and
improvement of life, but are also revelations of the very
structure of reality, so that ideals are more real than
atoms, and are even more truly objective and independent of man than is the Milky Way. Persons who think
thus are usually called philosophical idealists. Others,
granting the practical need of ideals in human life, view
them as being transitory products of a universe which in
reality is quite indifferent to ideals. These persons are
called materialists or mechanists. There is another party
of those who say that they regard the problem of the
nature of the universe as too difficult for speculation and
they call themselves agnostics; but the needle's point of
complete agnosticism is too difficult a balancing place for
a human mind; and practically agnostics accept either
an idealistic or a materialistic position. The history of
thought is in the main the history of idealism versus
materialism.

It seems most presumptuous for an individual to seek to
decide this ancient feud or even to take sides where the
greatest minds differ. Yet the fact of human life is that
this is one of the questions on which taking sides is a
necessity because suspension of judgment is itself a de-

cision — against idealism, namely. Not only is a decision necessary, but it is also of supreme importance; for, while both schools recognize ideals, they do not recognize the same ideals, nor is the faith and confidence of humanity in its own future and in the value of life nourished alike by each.

Are ideals real? Do they reveal reality which is permanent and dependable and beyond man? First appearances are strongly against idealism. H. C. King rightly points out the seeming unreality of the spiritual life. Beauty is fragile; and the noblest idealist falls prey, perhaps to accident or disease, certainly to death. But the persistent idealist believes that even " the hazards of finite selfhood " (as Bosanquet has called them) may reasonably be viewed as having meaning for the ideal order of the universe.

It is not my purpose here to enter into the technical arguments for idealism. I aim only to show, by a brief consideration of a few recent and contemporary writers, that those thinkers who most emphatically reject idealism nevertheless, in one way or another, reassert its cardinal principle.

Let us take, for instance, Friedrich Nietzsche. He is a thinker of whom many Americans heard for the first time during the World War. He was depicted, along with Treitschke and Bernhardi (two minds very different from his, although Bernhardi quoted him), as an unprincipled wretch, who favored war at any price. The insanity of the last dozen years of his life was played up

against him. He was called " Nietzsche the monster," as
he had signed himself in his pitiful delirium. He was
said to teach the crudest doctrine of " might makes right."
His ethics, derived from Darwinism (as Mr. Bryan was
aware), was based on the struggle for existence and the
survival of the fittest. Did he not say, " love peace only
as means to new wars " ? Did he not teach that " a good
war hallows any cause " ? Did he not assail the Christian
ethic of love and pity? Did he not proclaim that God
was dead? In short, was he not a destroyer of all ideals,
who would substitute for them the reign of ruthless force?
Everyone who had not read him, and some who had,
regarded him with a revulsion little short of horror.

In war days most Americans shared in accepting this
picture of Nietzsche. It is true that the elements of the
picture were elements of Nietzsche's thought; but as they
were depicted they almost completely misrepresented
him. The doctrine that the whole is more than the sum
of its parts is nowhere truer than in the understanding of
any human person, especially so complex a person as
Nietzsche. He was, indeed, in revolt against the ideals
of contemporary Christendom, which he regarded as weak
and slavish in spirit — *Sklavenmoral!* The culture of
the age seemed to him petty. These ideals, this culture,
he wished if possible to destroy. Democracy and the
dominant religion both seemed to him dispiriting and
enervating. He speaks of the two great European nar-
cotics, alcohol and Christianity. But he was not a mere
destroyer of ideals, fiercely as he thundered. He was

the prophet of new tables of values, with a prophetic consciousness — " Thus spake Zarathustra." He had a vision of a possible humanity, free, strong, creative, individual, so far above man that " as the ape is to man, so will man be to superman — either a joke or a sore shame." Man is a bridge to something better than man. The strength of the superman of the future is no mere brute force; it is spiritual achievement and personal independence. When Nietzsche counseled the loving of peace as means to new wars, he meant no national policy. He was speaking of the restless urge and inner struggle of man's spirit toward that which is higher and stronger. " Let your work be a struggle, your peace a victory." In other words, " fight the good fight with all thy might." When he attacked Christian love and pity, it was because he was fearful that they encouraged spiritual lethargy. Not *Nächstenliebe,* love of the neighbor, the nearest, but *Fernstenliebe,* love of the most distant, the ideal man of the future, should animate us.

Far from being a materialistic jingo, Nietzsche was an open foe of nationalism and was a political idealist. The very word " Deutsch," " German," in his writings was almost a term of contempt, much as is the word " American " in the writings of an H. L. Mencken. The ideal of nationalism revolted him. The state " is the coldest of all cold monsters " and " is the slow suicide of all." Nietzsche looked " beyond all these national wars, new empires, and whatever else is in the foreground; what concerns me, for I see it slowly emerging, is the One Europe."

The unity of Europe will be caused partly by the broad and international outlook of the Superman. Such types anticipating him as have appeared — Napoleon, Goethe, Beethoven, Stendhal, Heine, Schopenhauer, Wagner (to whose name he attaches a "perhaps") — were, he says, nationalists only in their weaker hours. Further, as he acutely observes, economic necessity will lead to the unity of Europe. Instead of being the advocate of *Deutschland über alles* he was more nearly a protagonist of the committees of the League of Nations on Economic and Intellectual Cooperation. But no; his soul abhorred all committees, and he would have the new day come by strong individuals rather than by organizations.

He rejected God and immortality — for most men the source and expression of the highest ideals. But he had faith in the attainability and reality of ideals, which he embodied in his extraordinary doctrine of the recurrence of all things, " Der ewige Wiederkehr." The universe, according to this theory, repeats itself in cycles. The highest values, therefore, are never destroyed and we should so live that we could wish to have our life repeated an infinite number of times. It is easy to pick flaws in the logic of this fancy and show that it leads to hopeless fatalism rather than to hope of eternal value; but this logical criticism does not affect the fact that Nietzsche intended it to embody his faith in the permanent ideal movement of reality.

There is no doubt, we freely admit, that Nietzsche meant to attack the ideals currently held and that he

made serious errors of judgment in so doing.   But he was
far from being a materialist.   While intending to attack
idealism, he was himself a militant and fanatical idealist
who took his ideals more seriously than most of his better
balanced and saner fellow creatures.   From him we may
learn to form a higher estimate of the possibilities of personality and a deeper respect for individuals.   Hear him
utter his reverence for personality in poetic lines,

> " Too nigh, my friend my joy doth mar, —
> I'd have him high above and far,
> Or how can he become my star? "

From him we may learn, as from the psychologists, the
perils of false ideals.   But above all he reveals to us the
fact that a great mind may, in the interests of a passionate
faith in ideals, reject the conventional forms of idealism
and still believe that the world is such that it can and
ought to produce great personalities with titanic energy
and lofty dreams.[18]

A very different sort of thinker is George Santayana,
the most polished man of letters among living philosophers.[19]   He is more sophisticated, more critical, less
passionate than Nietzsche; but like him he is essentially
a poet.   In his metaphysics Santayana is a materialist.
The physical world for him is physical, and no more is to
be said about it.   For him it is neither the deed of a God
nor the creation or expression of any spirit.   In its structure there is only matter.   Ideals have no part in it.   Thus
far the account of the universe is the dull tale common to
all materialists.

But a perusal of his writings shows that, again like all materialists, he was human before he was materialistic; and human beings are necessarily ideal-forming creatures. Santayana's real life is not lived in the world of matter which his philosophy would have us take to be the whole reality, but rather in the world of his ideal imaginings. In reality, as his theory describes it, there is no goodness or beauty or God or immortality. But in the world of ideal essences, he finds goodness and beauty on which his mind may feast and delight itself; yes, he is able to find in the words God and immortality symbols of the values which he discovers in that world. Symbols, yes; but mere symbols.

Santayana, therefore, lives in two worlds — the real world which is unideal and the ideal world which is unreal. Strange as it may sound, this is the practical solution at which many delicate spirits arrive. After the adventure of thought, they return to the *status quo ante,* the very dualism and contradiction which thought finds between the real and the ideal and which drives us on to search for truth. This is really the tribute which materialism pays to idealism — the acknowledgment that ideals are to be respected, yet that there is no way of finding a place for them in the world which materialism defines. This is what must happen when one's view of reality is built on a fraction of experience only. Sense experience is very important. It introduces us to certain aspects of the real world. Only a sentimentalist would try to ignore it. But important as is sense experience,

experience of ideals is still more important, for only when sense experience is interpreted by ideals does it reveal to us the structure of a world. Santayana, like many others, constructs his view of what is truly real out of objects given only to sense-perception. Only after having thus framed a world in which ideals have no place does he discover the importance of ideals. The idealist believes that such a procedure is artificial; he would regard it as more reasonable to build one's view of reality out of all the materials which reality gives us. He would, therefore, not try to decide what the real world is on the basis of the evidence of the senses merely, but would take into account our whole range of ideal value-experience too. Matter and mind, frustration and fulfilment, datum and whole mind, things and ideals — all of these must find some explanation in the nature of what is real. In the end, thought must go either with Santayana or with the idealists. Either the real world is material and the ideal is pure imagination; or else the real world itself embodies an ideal order and meaning. Santayana's view, like all materialism, leaves the very existence of ideals, even as imaginations, a mystery. If the universe is unconscious matter, there is nothing about it to make the rise of ideals intelligible. The idealist's view includes experience as a whole. Santayana goes halfway, and points out the facts which must be considered, but leaves them lying side by side unrelated to each other.

In many other thinkers, the same movement may be traced. Ideals are thrown out of the door. They come back in through the window. Democritus, the Greek atomist, makes reason the test of truth, and so one historian has called him " the first great idealist," although he was a materialist. The Syrian essayist, Lucian, poked fun at the philosophies and religions of his day, most of which needed it. He called Jesus a crucified Sophist, and ridiculed the gullibility of Christians. Yet this " second-century Voltaire " — like him of the eighteenth century — lived and died loyal to the ideals of honesty and truth as he saw them. Perry, the new realist of our own day, rejects every moral and spiritual ontology and yet trusts reality to render possible the continuing progress of humanity. John Dewey repudiates idealism and traditional religion but gives himself to the service of humanity and educational advance.

Every thinker who is true to human nature, then, trusts certain great ideals which he finds in his reflective experience. But the realists and materialists trust them half-heartedly when it comes to thinking about the nature of the cosmos. They are unwilling to see in them any clew to what the real universe is. For them, ideals may be guides to action but not to truth. The idealists, however, trust them whole-heartedly. They see in true ideals the basic laws of what the universe is and is becoming. Matter can be judged by ideals; ideals cannot be judged by matter. Mere ideals, then, are the very stuff and fabric of the universe and idealizing mind is the source and end of all things.

The function of ideals is to interpret the datum that we

experience. Interpretation is telling what things mean, by discovering what our own experience means. Interpretation means transformation, both theoretical and practical, yet without loss of identity.

Despite the difficulties and misunderstandings which arise, idealism has continued through the centuries at its task of transforming the world. Many think that this transformation should be purely practical and not theoretical. Use ideals, they counsel, to make the world better; but do not trust them to tell what the world is. Let us hope for human progress, but let us rely on no spiritual factor in reality, no power of ideals beyond us, no God. This humanism is the chief intellectual foe of idealism at the present time. Names like John Dewey, George Santayana, Bertrand Russell, R. B. Perry, Durant Drake, M. C. Otto, and many others belong in the humanistic group: all men who are devoted to ideals, yet repudiate idealism. These men think that ideals are alien to the real world in which they arise, the natural laws of which they interpret, the environment of which they so freely reshape.

Idealism must continually reinterpret itself and its world to every new generation in the light of new facts and the historical movements of the age. This age has inclined to put the meaning of life into biological terms and to define it as the adaptation of human organisms to their environment. But since the organism is active and farseeing, it is better to speak of the adaptation of the environment to the organism. Yet, since the meaning of

the whole process is not in any physical arrangement of
the material particles of either organism or environment,
it is truest of all to say that the aim of life is the adaptation of organism and environment to ideals revealed in
conscious experience. If this be so, much of what is regarded as very practical is truly impractical; and " mere "
idealism, the exploration and use of ideals, is a most
practical task for the human race.

CHAPTER VI

IDEALISM AS A CONTEMPORARY PHILOSOPHY

Thus we have considered the fundamental principles of an idealistic philosophy, as it confronts mind, nature, and ideals, and have weighed some of the typical objections to " mere idealism." It is now natural to raise the question as to whether such a philosophy is an actual force in the modern world. There are those who regard idealism as utterly out of date. They will grant that it has a certain logical plausibility, but they hold that it has been superseded by newer modes of thinking. Much criticism of this sort rests on the unfortunate assumption that philosophy is only a matter of fashion. If idealism be true, its popularity or unpopularity can neither add to nor subtract from its truth. But a brief consideration of the status of idealism as a contemporary philosophical system will perhaps help us to understand it and to estimate it more justly.

By contemporary idealism is meant idealism in the period from 1910 to the present. The year 1910 is not chosen arbitrarily. For American philosophy, at least, that year is a turning point. The period for some quarter of a century or more before it had been dominated by the figures of James and Royce at Harvard; while Bowne at Boston, standing somewhat magisterially apart from his professional colleagues and largely ignored by them, nevertheless exerted a profound influence on thousands. Royce and Bowne were idealists, and Royce regarded James's pragmatism as an empirical idealism under Kantian influence.[1] In 1910 James and Bowne both died. By that year Royce had done his chief work, although numerous significant writings were yet to issue from his pen. The time of the three great men had passed, and a new time had dawned. A group of the younger philosophers issued in that same year " The Program and First Platform of Six Realists," polemically directed against idealism which they recognized as " the dominant philosophy of the day." Idealism was thus challenged by a realism which, however sincerely it disavowed naturalism, was grounded in the categories of mathematics and natural science. This movement had been presaged in America by the founding of the *Journal of Philosophy, Psychology, and Scientific Methods* in 1904, as a friendly rival to the *Philosophical Review*.[2] The new realism was provided with its scriptural authority in this critical year, 1910, by the publication in England of Whitehead and Russell's *Principia Mathematica*.[3] In Germany, also in this year, Natorp opened his neo-Kantian *Grundlagen der exakten Wissenschaften* [4] with the statement that relations between the sciences and philosophy were becoming much closer. We may comment that the sciences were in the asymmetrical relation of swallowing to philosophy. Under the influence of the spirit of the times, the moral, esthetic, spiritual, and in some instances even the logical values cherished by idealism were taken out of its hands and given over to anthropology, history, sociology, and psychology. More serious, perhaps, because more fundamental and far-reaching in its consequences, psychology itself was given over to biology; and behaviorism, ably seconded by neo-realism, banished consciousness itself. The outlook for idealism seemed dark.

As we now review in retrospect what in 1910 was prospect only, and a dismal prospect, we shall group our reflections about three main centers: first, the remarkable vitality of idealism; secondly, the definition of idealism and its types; and thirdly, an account of the main characteristics of idealism in the period from 1910 to the present.

I

The vitality of idealism in the recent past is one of the most remarkable facts of recent philosophical development. It is remarkable because, despite the situation in 1910, despite G. E. Moore's famous and subtle " Refutation of Idealism," written in 1903,[5] and despite the attacks to which idealism has been subjected at the hands of pragmatic, instrumentalist, neo-realistic, and radical empirical opponents, it has both survived and grown. Indeed, today one may say that idealism is more vigorous and its position more secure than in 1910.

The leaders of philosophical thought in Germany dur-

ing the recent past have been Eucken, Rickert, Windelband, and the neo-Kantians — all, in some sense, idealists, unless we except positivists like Riehl. The chief
Italian philosophers of international fame were the neo-
Hegelians, Croce, Gentile, and Varisco, and Aliotta, whose
thought has passed through changing phases. Bergson,
the outstanding figure in French philosophy, although
hard to classify, is in the broad sense an idealist, influenced by the personalist Renouvier. Hamelin was an
avowed personalist. In England idealism has continued
its tradition of productivity under the leadership of Bernard Bosanquet, the second edition of whose *Logic* appeared in 1911 and whose two volumes of Gifford Lectures
on *Individuality and Destiny* were published in 1912 and
1913. One need only mention James Ward, M'Taggart,
Rashdall, Pringle-Pattison, Sorley, and A. E. Taylor to
suggest varied contributions to idealistic thought. Special
reference should be made to N. K. Smith's *Commentary
on Kant's Critique of Pure Reason,* and also to his in-
augural address as successor of Pringle-Pattison at
Edinburgh, "The Present Situation in Philosophy."[6]
In this address, N. K. Smith declared that "idealism,
now as hitherto, is probably the philosophy of the great
majority of men." R. F. A. Hoernlé, although now
geographically remote in South Africa from centers of
philosophical thought, keeps on interpreting idealistic
principles.

The literary activity of idealism in America has also
been vigorous, as may be indicated by reference to such

names as W. E. Hocking, G. P. Adams, and H. B. Alexander; or to the volume of essays in honor of James Edwin Creighton (1917), or to Royce's posthumous *Lectures on Modern Idealism,* edited by J. Loewenberg in 1919, or to the presidential addresses at the American Philosophical Association by M. W. Calkins in 1918 and by H. B. Alexander in 1919.   R. T. Flewelling has written several works popularizing personalistic idealism, and in 1920 founded *The Personalist,* a quarterly which survives in full vigor.   R. A. Tsanoff's *The Problem of Immortality* [7] is an independent product of idealistic thought.   H. W. Carr, the British philosopher, who has for some time been writing in behalf of a neo-Leibnizian idealism, has now become a resident of America, in California, and continues his work there.   In 1926, G. A. Wilson's *The Self and its World* appeared, with its closely reasoned plea for personalism.[8]   A. C. Knudson's work, *The Philosophy of Personalism,*[9] published in 1927, bears eloquent testimony to the continued power of idealism to inspire great philosophical writing.

It is true that many of the idealists whom I have named belong to the older generation, and many (as was noted in Chapter V) no longer are alive.   Eucken, Windelband, Natorp, James Ward, Bosanquet, Bradley, M'Taggart, Rashdall, and Creighton are among the distinguished idealists who have died in recent years.   Yet there remain many representatives of idealistic thought, and not a few of them are of the so-called younger generation.   Idealism is still a living and developing philosophy.

II

Up to the present point in this volume we have usually called any philosophy idealistic if it embodied the reasoned conviction that ideals somehow belong to the very objective structure of the universe. Without forgetting that many types of philosophy are idealistic in this broad sense even though they may not call themselves idealistic, it should be remembered that idealism as a specific school of philosophy has made and is making important characteristic contributions to philosophy.

But what is idealism as a specific school? " Philosophy as the Art of Affixing Labels " aroused the righteous antagonism of the late J. E. Creighton.[10]   Nevertheless labels there must be if men are to understand each other; only it is important that the labels mean something, that they be clear and true descriptions of that to which they are affixed. Is " idealism " such a label? We have affixed it to Natorp and Bergson, G. P. Adams and M'Taggart, Bosanquet and James Ward. If these are equal to the same thing, idealism, they assuredly are not equal to each other. Whatever idealism may be, if we are right in calling these men idealists, it is a very catholic and inclusive thing, a sort of Messianic Age in which the lion and the lamb lie down together. The question, What is idealism? is difficult and urgent, but at the same time it threatens to evaporate into triviality. For it appears that if you succeed in defining it, you will have devised a label which means everything and therefore means nothing.

Neo-realism itself turns into idealism; for, in a sense, Perry's meliorism, and, in another sense, Spaulding's neo-realism of ideals are both idealistic. If Saul is also among the prophets, what becomes of prophecy?

However, the historic difficulty with the term idealism has not been its meaninglessness, but rather its over-rich multiplicity of meanings. Perhaps we may best arrive at a concept of the genus idealism (if such there be) by a consideration of some of the various particular types of meaning that have been attached to the term.

If we consult that being indispensable to the philosophical vivisector, the man on the street, he will be able to give us a description of his notion of what an idealist is. He will picture the dreamer of the ought-to-be who ignores the is, the follower of the gleam, the seer of " the light that never was, on sea or land," hence (descending to his own vocabulary) an utterly impractical person, a " mere " idealist. It has been urged in a political convention that a certain candidate was a man of ideals " but not an idealist." Now technical philosophy should not admit ready-made, question-begging epithets into its collection of orthodox labels. To make idealist mean dreamer is to deprive the word of any special force. Again, the concept of idealist as that of anyone who believes in ideals is altogether too vague. The class of believers in ideals is much too broad to be significant. The class of believers in ideals would include everyone who in any sense longs for, desires, admires, or approves any status or object in the universe other than his present

situation; for this other status or object would in some
sense be an ideal for him. Thus every human being in
his senses would be an idealist.

Philosophical idealists have believed something much
more specific and have often conceived of ideal values as
being more than objects desired; as having, indeed, some
sort of objective existence in the real universe which conferred meaning on the desires directed toward them; an
existence not in the world of space and time, but in some
transcendent realm or order of eternal being. This idealism, a belief in the objectivity of value, is held in varying
senses and degrees by thinkers in our period such as
Bosanquet, G. P. Adams, Hocking, Pringle-Pattison, and
Sorley. We might well denominate this the Platonic type
of idealism, without attributing a complete Platonism to
its modern representatives. It is worth while at this point
to emphasize again the fact that Spaulding's anti-ideal-
istic *New Rationalism* is, in the end, a form of Platonic
idealism.

It might be thought that the definition of the Platonic
type is adequate as a definition of idealism in general.
This would be most natural for those to believe who accept the neo-realistic dogma that idealism is absolute
optimism; for absolute optimism is objectivity of values
with a vengeance. But not only may one believe in the
objectivity of values without being an absolute optimist
(witness Spaulding), just as one may believe in the objectivity of nature without being a naturalist; but also
one may be an idealist, of a very important type histori-

cally and contemporaneously, without belief in the objectivity of values, or at least without making that belief the logical center of gravity for one's thought. Ask any young student of philosophy what idealism is and he will ordinarily say nothing of the objectivity of values. He will speak rather of the theory that reality is throughout of the nature of consciousness, or at least that everything knowable is of that sort. One or both of these conceptions is central in the thinking of Berkeley, Hume, Mill, Kant, Fichte, Hegel, Schopenhauer, Lotze, and many others, including a neo-Hegelian like Croce, but not Bosanquet or Creighton. The presence of Hume and Schopenhauer on the list proves that belief in objectivity of value is not always associated with this type of idealism. The predominant interest of the type in consciousness, based largely on the influence of Descartes and Locke, received its chief classical formulation in Berkeley. Hence we shall call this type the Berkeleian. The name is not intended to impute to others than Berkeley either his empiricism or his metaphysics; but it may serve to point out what, in the modish, up-to-the-minute jargon, would be styled their common " mentalism."

Thus far we have arrived at two types of idealism, the Platonic and the Berkeleian. These two types are not quite identical with the two designated Platonic and Berkeleian by Edward Caird;[11] they are, however, closely related to what he appears to intend. But that even Caird's authority would not justify us in regarding this classification as exhaustive (if it was so designed) is evident to any reader of Caird himself, or of Creighton's well-known article on " Two Types of Idealism," [12] wherein he draws clear distinctions between the Berkeleian mentalism and " speculative philosophy." The latter label was suggested by Bosanquet as a substitute for the older term, " absolute idealism."

Now a question might arise as to whether the speculative philosophy would not better be classified as of the Platonic type, expressing, as it does, a belief in the objectivity of value. " The characteristic mark of idealism " (in this sense), says Creighton, " as it is found in the great systems, is its direct acceptance of things as having value or significance." Strictly speaking, then, absolute or speculative idealism is a species of the genus Platonic. But for two reasons it may be well classified as a separate type: first, because it is so stately and so influential a form of idealism that it would be unhistorical to deny it a separate rubric; and secondly, because, although it equates value and existence and thus maintains the objectivity of value, in that very act it empties value of specific meaning; to make the absolute totality of all experience the one and only value in the true sense is very near to destroying the value of value in concrete, finite lives. At best, as Perry has well pointed out, the outcome is " a monism of values," a " reduction of other values to one value," namely, systematic unity or coherence, which, quoting again, " looks suspiciously as though it were dictated by the facts of nature." [13] Because of the unique theory of value as logical coherence, total organic unity in a universe where everything is internally related, we are justified in making a third category of " speculative philosophy " and systems related to it, such as Kantianism and neo-Kantianism.   N. K. Smith's *Commentary* has shown that the modern coherence theory has its roots in Kant.   This type, then, might be called logical or organic idealism, or Hegelianism.

At least one other idealism is still out in the cold.   I mean that in which the self or personality is the basic interest.   Here, again, the classification does not sharply dissever the type from other types.   Plato himself never forgot the soul; Berkeley recognized no ideas save for spirit; M'Taggart and M. W. Calkins, for instance, are organic idealists profoundly interested in the self as ultimately real.   On the other hand, one may be a Platonic idealist, like Spaulding, or a Berkeleian, like Hume, or a speculative philosopher, like Bosanquet, and regard the finite self as something to be explained in terms of notself, or to be somehow transcended in ultimate reality. This fourth type of idealism, which may be called the personalistic, is thus sufficiently distinct to stand by itself.[14]

Personalistic idealism, in the broad sense, has two chief roots, the epistemological and the moral.   The epistemological motif comes from the Kantian emphasis on the activity of the self in knowing which is prominent in the thought of many philosophers, such as Lotze, T. H. Green, Bowne, and many others.   The moral motif comes also from Kant, being derived from the doctrine of the primacy of the practical reason.   Only persons can be moral; and one who is rationally led to accept the objectivity of moral values is easily inclined to the view that such values can be objective only in an order of personal reality. A personalist finds a necessary relation between the Platonic and the Berkeleian types of idealism; for how can values be objective if not, as T. H. Green puts it, " for, of, or in a person " ? Since Lotze illustrates both the epistemological and the moral aspects, personalistic idealism may be described as Lotzean.

There are, then, at least four main types of idealism. The first, the Platonic, asserts the objectivity of value. The second, the Berkeleian, holds that all knowable reality, and perhaps all reality *überhaupt,* is of the nature of consciousness. The third, the Hegelian, points to the coherence of one absolute system as the only true value or existence. The fourth, the Lotzean, finds in selfhood or personality an ultimate fact of fundamental significance. These are the great idealisms. What then is the long-sought-for definition of idealism? Is there a common element in the four types? I must confess that I find it difficult to detect any such element. The concluding paragraph of Bosanquet's *Logic* comes near to solving the problem. " The ' driving force of Idealism,' as I understand it, is not furnished by the question how mind and reality can meet in knowledge, but by the theory of logical stability, which makes it plain that nothing can fulfil the conditions of self-existence except by possessing the unity which belongs only to mind." [15] But this is not wholly fair to the epistemological motif of personalism, nor to some forms of Platonic idealism. In short, it is merely a broad definition of the speculative philosophy of Bosanquet. It would be safer to admit that it is impossible to define the generic term idealism with precision. If we proffer consciousness as the common element, we find some idealists of the unconscious; if we suggest mind, we find some idealists recognizing a nature not reducible to mental status; if we point to a common interest in personality, we are confronted with many cases of impersonal idealism which refuses to regard finite or any other personality as ultimate.

Nevertheless we shall have a vague working definition if we say that all idealism is characterized by belief in the ultimate reality or cosmic significance either of mind (using the term in the broadest sense) or of the ideals and values revealed to and prized by mind. The term idealism is so embedded in the history of philosophy that the attempt to eradicate it made by Bosanquet is probably destined not to succeed. But if intelligibility is desirable, it is imperative to qualify the noun by some adjective like Platonic or Berkeleian or speculative (or neo-Kantian) or personalistic.

III

We are now ready to undertake our third task, that of giving some account of the main characteristics of the idealism (or rather of the idealisms) of the period from 1910 to the present. We shall call attention first, to the struggle with realism; secondly, to the peculiar fate of

epistemology; thirdly, to the sharpening of the distinction between speculative philosophy and personalism;
and fourthly, to the increased emphasis on the philosophy
of values.

First, then, we turn to the struggle with realism. American neo-realism was, as we have seen, formally launched
in 1910. It is, on the face of it, hostile to every type of idealism. Mind, it asserts, is in no sense ultimate, nor have
values cosmic significance or objectivity (save for Spaulding and, perhaps, Montague). What we have called mind
or consciousness may be shown by analysis to be in reality a highly complex system of external relations among
terms themselves neither mental nor conscious, but (famous new label!) " neutral." Of these homeless subsist-
ents (orphans, and proud of it, spurning all asylums),
entities which do not even exist, but are mere candidates
for existence, the realistic universe of being is made up.
Now the status of a candidate is notoriously obscure; but
out of this obscurity matter and mind are made up. If
mind fare thus, values, being dependent on mind, are still
further from the realm of the truly real. Thus runs the
tale of the predominant tendency in American neo-
realism. Spaulding and Montague would of course reject
various items in this account, but most of the school
would probably accept most of the points mentioned.

Apparently there is no peace between such a tendency
and idealism of any type. Neo-realism has attacked the
Platonism of an objective order of spiritual values, the
Berkeleianism of consciousness as a philosophical ulti-

mate, the organic theory of truth of absolute idealism, and the metaphysical significance of the self or personality. Not a shred of idealism remains! Neo-realism proclaims itself as a new dogmatism, the ultimate metaphysic, the scientific philosophy, in opposition to the romanticism and paradox of all idealism. Even so moderate and temperamentally idealistic a " realist " as J. E. Boodin, who eschews " neo "-realism, joins in the charge that " idealistic systems have, one and all, been romantic exaggerations." [16]

Idealism has met these attacks with numerous counter-attacks, asserting, *inter alia,* that realism is itself a highly artificial conceptual construction, and therefore presupposes some sort of idealism; that its analytic method, while valuable, is not, even when supplemented by synthesis, adequate to a knowledge of wholes or values, since they demand a method of intuition and hypothesis or what Sorley calls a synoptic view. Realism is said to be an abstract and partial interpretation of the data, aiming, as it does, at the lowest terms of analysis instead of at the richest and most comprehensive unity of experience; it is also criticized for assuming the final and absolute truth of the present results of the mathematical and natural sciences, being, as has been said by one idealist, more reverential of science than the scientists themselves.

It is impracticable for us to review this debate in the space at our disposal. But two items in the situation should be specified: first, the antihistorical spirit of neo-realism, and secondly, the realistic return to idealism.

The first point, the antihistorical spirit of neo-realism, may appear unfairly stated. It is true that the spirit of neo-realism may only with reservations be described as antihistorical. Marvin has written a *History of European Philosophy*. Perry and Spaulding have devoted themselves to the exposition and criticism of the main types of philosophical thought. Others have made historical contributions. The volume *The New Realism* [17] opens with an interesting account of the historical relations of neo-realism. Despite all this, we are describing its spirit as antihistorical. For, speaking broadly, the school's verdict is that the history of philosophy is on the wrong track, or, if you please, entirely off the track and wandering in the wilderness. One who reads the neo-realistic literature comes away with the impression that most of Plato, practically all of Aristotle, certainly all of Plotinus, Descartes (except his saving mathematics), Berkeley (unless he was a realist in disguise), Kant, Hegel, and Lotze, Bergson, Bradley, and Bosanquet, all and one, root and branch, are misleading and erroneous. Only certain aspects of Plato, Hume, and Herbert Spencer are the recipients of good words. To substantially the entire history realism says, as no other important philosophical school has said, " vanitas vanitatum " and " mene, mene, tekel, upharsin; " yet to the present moment of mathematical science it cries, " Verweile doch, Du bist so schön." This attitude is not wholly to be condemned. It aims to substitute a direct analysis of the given, a grappling with the facts at first hand, for the traditional approach to every question *via* Plato and Aristotle, Kant and Hegel. But the value in this fresh first-hand study of the problems is not obviously contingent on a rejection of the history. The realistic tendency is extreme. The volume *The New Realism* is impatient and unappreciative of the philosophical tradition. It pleads for the separation of philosophical research from the study of the history of philosophy (pp. 29, 30) — a separation which most idealists would regard as opening the way for needless blunders in research and for a blind and barren type of historical study. The book indulges in questionable interpretations of Berkeley and Kant, discards " the entire British and Kantian psychology, together with all modern disguised variations " (p. 402), specifies " neo-Hegelian imbecilities " (p. 347), and in general reflects the spirit of G. E. Moore's " Refutation of Idealism," which asserts that " all philosophers and psychologists also have been in error " on the point in which he refutes idealism.

Idealism, with its more tolerant and catholic attitude, with its synthetic interpretation of the history, has at least a cultural advantage over a view which proclaims apocalyptically that the truth which ye seek has suddenly come to the temple (and destroyed it) about A.D. 1910. The doubts raised by this situation are such that the most cogent mathematical logic cannot quite still them. If the age-long struggle of human thought has been utterly deceived by its own illusions, it is hard to believe that the present is quite immune to self-deception. The *lex continui* obtains also in the history of philosophy.

The second special point in this connection was the realistic return to idealism. To see any such return may require the customary optimistic romanticism of the idealist. The situation makes at first the impression of a Babel of tongues. It is not so much that realism and idealism contradict each other as that, in certain respects, they are unintelligible to each other. Especially is this true of the theory of consciousness.

In general, neo-realism has adopted the theory that consciousness is behavior. Now believers in consciousness and behaviorists are always talking past each other. One group speaks of thought, feeling, will, awareness; the other speaks of the responses of an organism to stimuli. But unfortunately both groups insist on using some of the same terms; although J. B. Watson admits, as a consistent behaviorist, that he does not know what is meant by the terms consciousness, perception, attention, will, and the like.[18] The result is an amazing failure to join issues. Each party uses terms in what the other party regards as a Pickwickian sense. Idealism has the advantage here of recognizing the value of behavioristic method; while behaviorism is intolerant of idealism.

There are, then, senses in which there is no realistic return to idealism. If there is such a return, it is not in the flesh, but in the spirit; and not in the entire spirit. But underneath the confusion, many points of contact are visible. Take the worst case, that of behaviorism itself. This means that what have been regarded as relations among environmental and biological entities look so much like what has been called consciousness that behaviorists cannot tell the difference. Idealists may either despair at the disappearance of consciousness, or triumph at its unexpected conquests in the objective order. Or take the fundamental analytic method of realism. It is a " New Rationalism "; it asserts, with explicit dogmatism, the objective validity of logic, and reduces the contents of our minds to " neutral entities " which " are all of such stuff as logical and mathematical manifolds are made of." [19]   A universe of logical concepts in logical-mathematical relations would appear to be a variety familiar to idealism, in one sense Platonic and in another Hegelian, though in no sense Berkeleian or personalistic. Realism denies that logic is " mental "; but this denial is probably less significant than its doctrine that logic is objective. Not only is logic objective; for one document of the school, Spaulding's *New Rationalism,* values also are objective. Spaulding avows a " neo-realism of ideals " akin to the Platonic belief in the eternal reality of justice and the Good. The radical difference between this view and the orthodox neo-realistic denial of a moral or spiritual ontology has not been sufficiently noticed.[20]   It is important enough to be described as a realistic return to idealism. Likewise Boodin's *Realistic Universe,* rejecting the tenets of neo-realism, expounds a realism that finds values ultimate constituents of the universal order, and S. Alexander, the English realist, seeks to conserve values; " realism," he says, " strips mind of its pretensions but not of its value or greatness." R. B. Perry has written a *General Theory of Value.* If we have not here

a return to idealism, we have at least an increasing interest on the part of realists in those " ethical and religious
motives " that, according to B. Russell, " have been on
the whole a hindrance to the progress of philosophy."
That is, Russell's mood does not wholly dominate the
school. A. N. Whitehead's recent books, *Science and the
Modern World* and *Religion in the Making,* have been
generally regarded as more akin to idealism than his
earlier writings.[21]

What wonder is it then that the realist McGilvary, on
reviewing *The New Realism,* commented that " there is
not such a sharp issue between realism and idealism as
most of us had supposed," or that Bosanquet, in his 1917
article in the *Philosophical Review,* was able to find some
common ground with realism, or that Sheldon's doctrine
of " productive duality " teaches that they may be
reconciled?

But there remains a conflict on a fundamental issue
out of which, in the opinion of a personalist, the troubles
chiefly arise, an issue on which realists differ with idealists scarcely more than idealists differ among themselves
— namely, the metaphysics of personality. The characteristics of idealism in the period since 1910 which remain
to be considered are all concerned with problems growing
out of this issue.

A second outstanding trait of the period in question is
what we have called the peculiar fate of epistemology,
which is closely related to the realist-idealist controversy
as well as to the metaphysics of personality. Epistemol-

ogy, or theory of knowledge, has been a central problem
of philosophy since Locke. Kant brought it even more
into the foreground. The word epistemology was probably coined by the idealist, J. F. Ferrier, about the middle
of the nineteenth century. There has always been a
certain ambiguity as to just what epistemology is, and
just what its relations to psychology, logic, and metaphysics are; but that a critical examination of the nature,
function, and validity of knowledge was an essential and
a logically prior part of philosophy had come to be a
commonplace of thought. This is illustrated by the fact
that when Bowne came to revise his *Metaphysics* in
1897–1898, he made it into two volumes — a *Theory of
Thought and Knowledge* and a *Metaphysics*.

Over against this situation is the present fact that epistemology is now in very bad standing, neo-realism and the
speculative philosophy uniting to *écraser l'infâme*. As
to neo-realism, witness Marvin's essay on " The Emanci-
pation of Metaphysics from Epistemology." The speculative philosophy is equally unambiguous. " In Logic,
as I understand it," says Bosanquet, " attempting to follow out at a long interval the practice of the masters,
there is no epistemology in the sense supposed." [22]
Creighton tells us that the speculative philosophy " falls
to work to philosophize . . . without any epistemological
grace before meat " (p. 522). Nevertheless, and here
lies the peculiarity of epistemology's peculiar fate, that
discipline both is and is not rejected. For neo-realism's
contribution to this confusion, we may cite Holt's state-

ment that his *Concept of Consciousness* is " primarily an essay in epistemology and empirical psychology " (p. 209). About Russell's epistemological distinction between knowledge by acquaintance and knowledge by description rages much debate in England. In the idealist camp, the subtitle of Bosanquet's *Logic* is *The Morphology of Knowledge*. And Creighton, speaking of speculative philosophy, says that " its logic and ideal of truth must be that of the concrete universal; so much is determined by the very form of experience " (p. 529). " There is only one thing that it is unable seriously to question: its own capacity to advance beyond any given limit; only one category that lies beyond criticism, and that is the category of intelligence " (p. 531). Out of their own mouths, neo-realists and speculative idealists are therefore convicted of a fundamental interest in the nature and function of knowledge. Why then do they reject epistemology?

At least three factors probably enter into this rejection. The first factor is the attempt apparently made by some epistemological philosophers to spin an entire metaphysics out of the sole data of theory of knowledge. Because the conditions of knowledge are what they are, these philosophers argue that reality must be of a certain kind. That this is a hasty and fallacious route to idealism or any other ontology was explicitly held by Bowne and would be universally conceded today. At the same time, this is not to deny the fact, obvious to most philosophers, that there is a close and unique relation between knowing and

being.   Indeed, one chief point in the speculative philosophy's attack on epistemology is the very fact that
problems of knowledge and of reality are too closely
intertwined to be separated.

The second factor is the artificial widening of the
chasm between thought and thing, of which some epistemology has been guilty.   The classical case of this
chasm is the doctrine of the *Dinge an sich,* which held
that the function of knowledge was not to know the things
themselves.   For it, knowing did not reveal, but concealed
the object.   This conception is an *überwundener Stand-
punkt,* except in positivistic circles.   It is the common
view of most idealists and realists that reality is knowable.   An epistemology of intimate relation between
thought and its objects has taken the place of that which
interposed a chasm between them.   The old epistemology
changes, giving place to new; but precisely to a new
epistemology.

The third factor is the attack on the activity of the
self in knowledge.   If there has been one constant element
in the major epistemological tradition, it has been that
all knowledge presupposes a unitary and active self.
Thus spake Berkeley, Descartes, and Leibniz; Kant and
probably Hegel; Ferrier and T. H. Green; Lotze and
Bowne; Sorley and M. W. Calkins.   But the speculative
philosophy of recent times substitutes for the activity of
the self the purely logical conception of the organic whole
of reality.   Neo-realism also assails the notion of the
activity of the self in knowledge, regarding the presence

of the self in the knowledge-situation as merely an " ego-centric predicament " from which thought may and should abstract. The general motto is *ego delendus est.* The theory of knowledge without a knower follows the psychology without a soul.

A consideration of the fate of epistemology has thus yielded two results. It has shown that the objection of our contemporaries to epistemology is not to epistemology itself as much as to the name, or, more fairly stated, to what is regarded as the wrong kind of epistemology. It has also shown that the most serious present departure from the historical achievements of epistemology is to be found in the current rejection of the activity of the self in knowledge.

This prepares us for a sketch of the third main characteristic of recent idealism, namely, the clearer differentiation between speculative philosophy and personalism.

It cannot be said that a lucid treatment of the problem of personality, finite or infinite, has characterized the history of philosophy. Kant's phenomenal and noumenal selves multiplied the problem and increased the woe. It was hard to tell what self Fichte was talking about. As to Hegel — there are the wings of interpretation, right and left, for you to choose from. Even Lotze was obscure. If you read the *Microcosmus* and the *Outlines of Philosophy of Religion,* you found much clear personalism; if you read the *Metaphysics* you felt that you were not far from impersonal Spinozism. Similar cross currents may be detected in T. H. Green, and in the eloquent but turgid passages of Eucken.

Prior to 1910, however, there had already been a development in the direction of a clarification of the problem. In England, Andrew Seth (Pringle-Pattison) wrote his influential little book *Hegelianism and Personality* (1887), which, together with the work of James Ward, pleaded for a clear-cut definition of personality. From a different angle, M'Taggart made his own contribution to this end. In America, Bowne, more successfully than anyone else, built up an explicit personalism; while others, notably Royce and M. W. Calkins, were interpreting the fundamental importance of the self in being. But despite these currents, there was still much uncertainty and fumbling in dealing with the self. Bradley's critique of the self, together with his Absolute that is not personal because it is personal and more, is symptomatic of the prevailing confusion.

By contrast, the situation since 1910 has been more promising. Many of the philosophers already mentioned continued their work — James Ward, M'Taggart, Royce and Miss Calkins, for example. Especially significant is the fact that the speculative philosophy seemed to become more clearly conscious of the need of differentiating itself from personalism, and of aligning itself with the logical-organic as opposed to the Berkeleian type of idealism. Bosanquet's volume on *The Value and Destiny of the Individual* (1913) is devoted to an attack on personalism and an exposition of a theory of the universe in which only the organic whole is of value. Creighton's article, from which we have frequently quoted, is aimed at distinguishing Berkeleian "mentalism" (and presumably any form of personalism) from the speculative philosophy. Hoernlé also discusses the issue in his *Studies in Contemporary Metaphysics* and in his *Idealism as a Philosophy*. In England, Pringle-Pattison's *Idea of God in Recent Philosophy* is a personalistic counterblast to Bosanquet, while Sorley's stately lectures, *Moral Values and the Idea of God,* are a less polemic argument for the dependence of all values on personality, and their objective reality in a divine personality. In 1918 the Aristotelian Society held a Symposium on the question, " Do Finite Individuals Possess a Substantive or an Adjectival Mode of Being? " in which Bosanquet, Pringle-Pattison, G. F. Stout, and Lord Haldane participated. The persistent interest in the problem is indicated also by the Symposium of 1919, " Can Individual Minds be Included in the Mind of God? " by Rashdall, Muirhead, Schiller, and D'Arcy. The neo-realistic polemic against the self should be mentioned as contributing to the sharpening of concepts.

The renewed study of the metaphysics of personality and the consequent clear distinction between personalism and both speculative and realistic impersonalism are significant chiefly because of the relation of our conception of personality to our understanding of what is for most idealists the deepest category of intelligence, namely, the category of value. This category is one of vital importance to every human thinker of whatever school of thought. It is hoped that the study of ideals in Chapter III of the present volume may clear the way for a better understanding of values.

Let us turn, then, to a consideration of the fourth and last characteristic of idealism in the recent past, namely, the emphasis on the problem of values. This emphasis is not confined to professed idealists, but is shared by many pragmatists and realists. Nor did it have its beginning in 1910. Modern interest in the problem is illustrated by the line: Kant, Lotze, Ritschl. It has been increasingly the center of discussion ever since the monographs of Ehrenfels and Meinong in 1893 and 1894. Höffding's *Philosophy of Religion* in 1906 was an important event in the history of the theory of value. In this country, the works of Münsterberg and Urban and the " Value Number " of the *Psychological Bulletin* appeared in 1909, significantly near the beginning of the period that we are interested in. Since then, theory of value has been the subject of much discussion in the periodicals and at the meetings of the American Philosophical Association. W. G. Everett's *Moral Values* [23] is a contribution to the ethical aspects, the writings of Hocking and Coe to the religious. To the studies of the neo-realists in this field reference has already been made. The Englishmen, Bosanquet, Pringle-Pattison, Sorley, Galloway, and others; the Italians, Croce, Gentile, and Varisco; the Germans, Eucken, Windelband, Rickert, Dilthey, and Spranger have all, from various standpoints, discussed the problem of values. Out of so much intellectual labor, some results ought to have been produced. We shall discuss a few only of these results in the light of the positions held by speculative philosophers and by personalists.

There are certain main lines of agreement between these groups. Both esteem the concrete, the fullest and richest interpretation of reality, as opposed to abstractions such as those of which neo-realism is fond. In fact, as others have seen, idealism is at this point tough-minded and thick, rather than tender-minded and thin.

Again, both speculative philosophy and personalism regard value as fundamental in knowledge and reality. Münsterberg viewed value as the basic *a priori* of every *a priori*. Royce quoted with approval Rickert's saying that " the ought is prior in nature to the real," and argued that a nonidealist cannot avoid defining his real world in terms of his ideal.[24] Sorley imparts a fuller meaning to the maxim which Lotze preached but did not practice, that " ethics is the true beginning of metaphysics."

The different idealisms also agree in the conviction that finite personality does not find in its empirical career alone any adequate account of the highest goods of life. Neither the datum-self nor the whole-self creates its own values. Value originates beyond the self. As N. K. Smith says, " the supreme concern of idealism is to show that the esthetic and spiritual values have more than a merely human significance " (p. 15). Anti-idealism is expressed in Bush's failure to see why human values are any less valuable because merely human.

A final point of agreement between the two idealisms is the fact that both, in their deeper intention, seek to preserve the values of finite personality itself, as well as the objective values with which it is concerned.

These points are accompanied by divergences so great that the agreements might appear, and do appear to some, to be merely verbal. But after all, only a harsh and dogmatic school orthodoxy would deny that the two types of idealism have a common interest in the objectivity of value, to a considerable extent are animated by a common spirit, and come to some common conclusions. But, as we have said, the divergences are very great.

For speculative philosophy, the one and only true value, in and from which all finite persons derive their meaning, is the complete organic system of truth. This system is self-sufficient; it is not a person, nor does it exist for any person; all persons are finite fragments of it, the Whole. Personalism, too, holds that truth must be a consistent system; but it regards as irreducible the distinction between truth, which is a description of reality, and the reality described, which is the life of a society of persons. This society owes its existence and unity not alone to systematic coherence, but to the interrelations of finite personal wills and the underlying will of one Supreme Person. Personalism, then, would regard the professedly concrete system of speculative idealism as abstract, because it places system above personality, for which alone a unitary system of any kind has meaning. It makes personality subservient to system, instead of system's being subservient to personality.   Personalism finds value to consist not in an ultimately impersonal coherence to which persons are subordinated, but rather in a society of persons, attaining common purposes, and realizing common ideals; such that these purposes and ideals find their significance in being the expression and fulfilment of persons and what they ought to be. This is more than a difference in emphasis. It is a difference in standard of value, the difference that is vital to all theistic philosophy.

Perhaps it is only another way of stating the same idea to say that for speculative philosophy (as for neo-realism) logic is the discipline of chief metaphysical importance; whereas for personalism ethics is more significant than logic. Logic may with greater plausibility be stated in impersonal terms; ethics, however, has always to do with persons. If the world order is purely logical, speculative idealism may be true; if moral values are objective, personalism is probably true.

A final point of divergence turns on the problem of meaning and existence. Creighton's article best presents the case for the speculative philosopher. The category of existence, he argued, is not fundamental, but is a barren abstraction. " Meaning " (value) is rather the basic category, which is richer and includes existence. Thus far, he is asserting only ground common to the speculative philosopher and the personalist. But he interprets it to mean that mentalism, the interpretation of value in terms of psychic existence, is excluded. Now this appears to a personalist to go further than the assertion that meaning includes existence; it appears to reduce existence entirely to meaning. It is an abstraction of meaning from existence. For personalism, on the contrary, meaning and value always include a reference to personal existence of some sort. Not only is every meaning the act of a self; but that which it means is also wholly personal, namely, further acts of some selves or principles of their activity.

Personalism holds, as Sorley has in substance argued, that a value which does not exist is, as nonexistent, no value at all, and that the value of a value consists in some type of actual or possible embodiment in personal life, finite or infinite. Without existence, no value. Without personality, no existence. The personalist does not desire the self as an opportunity for intoning the blessed words " I am I," but rather as a medium in which to interpret and to develop a real and moral world order.

Our philosophical standpoint must meet the acid test: Does it justly interpret life as a whole? Does it envisage all the facts? Does it make all the facts intelligible? No philosophy comes out unscathed from this test. Our study may direct attention to the efforts of idealism to meet the conditions of the test. If we look ahead in the light of the recent history of thought, we may venture the opinion that the outlook for idealism, and for personalism in particular, is by no means unfavorable.

CHAPTER VII

TASKS CONFRONTING
CONTEMPORARY IDEALISM

Idealism is a living philosophy. Obviously, then, it is not a finished philosophy. What new forms it may assume in coming centuries one cannot venture to predict. Even the immediate future is uncertain. However, in a situation the outcome of which is uncertain, one may profitably consider what ought to be done. We therefore shall inquire into some of the tasks confronting an idealistic philosophy.

I

Among the odd misunderstandings prevalent among many writers of the present time is the notion that idealistic philosophy is conservative and static. A mechanistic or realistic or pragmatic philosophy is supposed to be vibrant with progress; whereas idealism is reactionary and bound to the past. The theory that the universe is made up of neutral entities is taken to be disillusioning and liberating; the theory that the universe is made up of minds and ideals is regarded as a sort of bondage. There is just enough truth in this grotesque caricature to give it some point. Idealism is probably more desirous of learning from the past and of conserving its permanent gains than are those recent philosophers who seem to believe that the human mind was wholly unenlightened before the year 1910.[1] Idealism may have exaggerated the logical unity and continuity of the history of human culture. It may have inclined to the extreme of holding that all serious thought and all genuine cultural experiences are in some sense true. But the contemporary reaction against the past has gone to the other extreme of holding that all past thought (except experimental science) and all civilization (except in so far as it was exclusively based on science) was in error.[2]

If one has to choose between these two extremes using contribution to progress as a principle of choice, it is all but self-evident that overemphasis on the contributions of the past is more likely to lead to permanent progress than is a complete ignoring of the past. The individual who constantly forgets his own yesterdays is abnormal. The individual who remembers them but can learn nothing from their experiences is not regarded as intelligent. Why, then, should a society forget its yesterdays or refuse to learn from them? Why should philosophy view the past as wholly on the wrong track? Is not idealism with its critical appropriation of the best in the past more likely to lead to new truth than is any philosophy which neglects the results of previous reflection? Building on a poor foundation is risky; but building on no foundation at all is even more risky. A philosophy founded on Plato has incomparably more chances of being right than a philosophy founded on J. B. Watson alone; for we have to go back to Plato through all the criticisms and constructions of the whole history of philosophy, whereas it is not self-evident that Watson has been through the history of philosophy at all.

There is, of course, danger of making a fetish of idealism as of any other " school." Against this danger Royce energetically warned philosophers.

" Hardly anything," he says, " is more injurious to the life of scholarship in general, and especially of philosophy, than the too strict and definite organization of schools of investigation. The life of academic scholarship depends upon individual liberty. . . . A philosophy merely accepted from another man and not thought out for one's self is as dead as a mere catalogue of possible opinions. . . . The inevitable result of the temporary triumph of an apparently closed school of university teachers of philosophy, who undertake to be disciples of a given master, leads to the devitalizing of the master's thought, and to a revulsion, in the end, of opinion." [3]

That there is a danger in all schools and traditions we may heartily agree, one that we minimize at our peril. Royce's wise words may well be taken to heart by realist (both new and critical) and instrumentalist, as well as by idealist. Allegiance to a philosophical or other tradition in any such fashion as to hamper individual initiative or free creativity would be calamitous so far as the intellectual life was concerned. " Ein jeder sollte nach seiner

Fasson selig werden." But while there is danger in the traditionalism of a "school" — whether Platonic or Watsonian, Democritean or Lotzean — one can hold no opinion whatever that does not have some relations to ideas held in the past. Where would the history of philosophy be but for the conscious allegiances of the great masters to their predecessors? — Socrates, Plato, Aristotle, Plotinus; the scholastics; the revivals of antiquity in the Renaissance; the English empiricists; the Cartesians, including Spinoza, Leibniz, and the schoolman of schoolmen, Wolff, who went to extremes but yet performed no mean service to his age; the Kantians, the Hegelians, the Lotzeans. How can one survey this history without seeing that it is no record of the individual insights of unique individuals, but the cooperative labor of free men not too free to learn from others? Eclecticism has always been regarded as on a lower intellectual level than the acceptance of some unified system; and the attitude that has nothing to learn from the past is on a still lower level. I do not see that idealists need apologize for having convictions. At any rate they may escape Santayana's scourge, " How, then, should there be any great heroes, saints, artists, philosophers, or legislators in an age when nobody trusts himself, or feels any confidence in reason, in an age when the word *dogmatic* is a term of reproach? " [4]

The charge, then, if it be a charge, that idealism esteems the past is well founded. If the universe is the activity of mind, then all history must reveal traces of the reason and truth of mind. But the other charge that idealism is conservative and hostile to progress is wide of the mark. It may be admitted that certain idealists have been political or social conservatives. Yet in so doing they have been untrue to the logic of idealism. Idealism is by its very nature both an appreciation and a critique of all existing institutions. The factual both reveals and conceals the absolute ideal. The idealist who sees the final revelation of the Absolute in the institutions of his own day and nation is refuted by his own logic of coherence. No existing institutions are " ideal." On the other hand, the logic of realism, and certainly of naturalism, points toward political realism, and perhaps toward the philosophy of force, even though many realistic and naturalistic philosophers happily do not draw the logical consequences from their conception of a universe which is indifferent to ideals.

This situation points clearly toward one imperative task confronting idealism: namely, the reassertion of its critical office and of its socially liberal and progressive logic. It has, however, strangely happened of late that John Dewey and Bertrand Russell have been uttering boldly the principles of social idealism which many professed idealists have failed to avow. By right of logic, social idealism is a necessary consequence of a metaphysical idealism which sees imperative ideals in the very structure of the universe. Idealistic philosophy, then, needs to revive its critical and progressive spirit, while retaining its discriminating appreciation of what has been.

II

But if idealists are to move forward as leaders in social and moral progress, it is of prime importance that they should be productive scholars. Without literary productivity, little influence; and without scholarship, literary activity will do more harm than good among the judicious. I am not pleading for an encyclopædic scholarship; no one has read everything, or has worked through every problem with equal thoroughness. Nor am I pleading for a technical scholarship more interested in formal accuracy than in vital meaning. But it is a fact that no philosophy can win or can maintain the respect of the thinking world without a basis of sound scholarship. Philosophy is no mere reciting of sound opinions; it is an interpretation of life in the light of all that logic and history and insight can furnish. Eucken, in spite of his turgidity, and James Ward, for example, have won a hearing by the sheer force of their scholarship. The interest of some idealists in life has perhaps tended to produce in some quarters an underestimate of the functions of scholarship. Of Hegel and Lotze, Royce and Bowne this was not true; and it need not be true at all. There is no incompatibility between serving the needs of human life and seeking to fulfil the high ideal of scholarship. It does, however, require a longer vision, a profounder faith in rationality and in the essential reasonableness of all persons in that society of which the Supreme Person is head and which is the universe. That

service which looks for immediate practical results may
not, in the end, be so practically useful to humanity as
that which loyally serves a more remote ideal.

Let these remarks not be misunderstood. They are
not a plea to substitute *Gelehrsamkeit* for insight, vo-
luminous reading for contact with life and reality. The
German ideal which makes scholarship largely a matter
of imperturbable patience in mastering detail is not the
whole truth about scholarship. But, if the remark that
Rudyard Kipling puts into the mouth of Kim that " the
more you know the better off you are " is true of anyone,
it is certainly true of those who aspire to scholarship in
philosophy. Only those who have examined the evidence
are entitled to an opinion in any matter; how much more
subtly true is this in the high emprise of philosophy! And
how important it is for a philosophy which would assume
the functions of social leadership to know what it is doing!
It is to furnish an enlightened view of the ends of human
living; carelessness here, even the substitution of en-
thusiastic good will for sound scholarship and rational
insight, is more serious than carelessness at any other
point.

III

It follows from what has been said that idealism can ill
afford to assume that its fundamental theoretical work is
completed and that, therefore, nothing remains save practical applications. The social prophet, with a burning
sense of injustice and with sympathy for suffering human-

ity, may be pardoned for underestimating the need of further philosophical inquiry. He may be pardoned; but he need not be believed. The idealist, then, like every true philosopher, must work on the unsolved problems of philosophy. "Unsolved problems" — what a vast field! There are two possible attitudes toward unsolved problems in philosophy. It may be asserted (as the neo-scholastics, the neo-realists, and the absolute idealists almost seem to assert) that substantially no problems are unsolved save matters of detail. On the other hand, it may be asserted that all problems are unsolved, and that in the nature of the case all that we may hope to do is to formulate the problems, leaving them forever as problems. Of these two attitudes the second is, of course, nearer to the truth than the first; and doubtless the neo-scholastics, the neo-realists, and the absolute idealists would resent my classification of them in the first group. Only an absolute mind could know absolute truth with absolute certainty. It may be that our mind is, in some respects, absolute; but one always wonders what the elephant (or tortoise) is standing on. None the less, the second is one that it is both impossible and unreasonable to maintain literally. If all problems are equally unsolved, then human life is in hopeless confusion. Bad as things are, they are not so bad as that. Some thoughts must be treated as truer than others; coherence must be regarded as truer than incoherence; some ideals as more worthy than others. Some of the problems about the fundamental structure of thought and reality must be regarded either as actually solved or as on the way to solution.

Such an attitude as this seems to be the proper one for idealism to assume. But suppose we accept all of the fundamental theses of idealism, or at least the great majority of them, as reasonably established, it would be the greatest mistake in the world to suppose that the only task of a teacher of philosophy was to impart those theses, to indoctrinate his students in the body of established truth, the new orthodoxy, much as a teacher of mathematics indoctrinates his students in the mathematical tradition. This mistake would lead to a stagnation of philosophical thought, a narrowing of interest, and a problem-blindness that would be fatal to further development. And the result would be almost equally fatal if the only addition to the indoctrination were polemics against opposing views; for there would still remain the peril of those same consequences. A great philosophical personality may perhaps with impunity make his life-work consist of just such indoctrination and polemic; a philosophical school, relying on intellectual and spiritual weapons alone, cannot remain vital without a keen sense of unsolved problems, of ever more pioneer work to do.

It is not my purpose in this connection to attempt any catalogue of the unsolved problems which still remain for an idealist. A few specimens may, however, be mentioned. The last word has not yet been said on the problem of freedom. The mind-body problem, the problems arising from abnormal psychology, the problems of social philosophy, including the relations of the individual to society and to the universe, are a nest of difficulties which must be faced. To pretend that final solutions have been found for them is folly; and the list given only scratches the surface of the situation. In order to give direction to the present discussion, let us turn our attention to four specific kinds of task that idealists must undertake if they are to do justice to the intellectual needs of the present. These four are first, historical investigation; secondly, systematic construction; thirdly, what may be called practical construction, although this is really only an aspect of the preceding; and fourthly, self-criticism.

First, then, we must give ourselves to historical investigation. We are living in an age whose historical consciousness is weak; an age dominated by science and hostile to tradition. Neo-realism, as I have elsewhere tried to show, may be flatly described as antihistorical in spirit. Even Bowne was less sympathetic with the study of the history of philosophy than he might have been, and James was even less so than Bowne. For a large number of contemporary philosophers, indeed, the history of philosophy began with William James, so that all thought is divided into the two categories: traditional (before James) and modern. This attitude may be the source of amusing historical errors, such as that committed in the Introduction to *The New Realism* which attributes to Toland the authorship of the stirring question, " If the trumpet gives an uncertain sound, who shall prepare himself to the battle? " When Toland penned that quotation little did he dream that his pages would ever fall under the eye of readers who would need to be told that St. Paul was the author of the words! But it is not such slips, which anyone in a careless moment might commit, that are the true basis of the case against indifference to the history of philosophy. Thorough indifference is the mother of complete ignorance; and complete ignorance of the history would reduce thought to barbarism, subject the present to all the errors that the past has lived through and overcome, deprive the present of all the insights that have made the past great, and make it impossible to understand the whence or the whither of contemporary currents of thought. Acquaintance with the thoughtful minds of the past, even though they may have been in error, is an intellectual and spiritual stimulus that no person of culture, not to say philosopher, can afford to lose. It is a foe to intolerance. Superficial knowledge of the history may indeed tend to skepticism; a profounder knowledge sees a rational meaning in the whole development. As Bacon sagely remarked, " A little philosophy inclineth man's mind to atheism, but depth in philosophy bringeth men's minds about to religion." The idealist should be the first to recognize these facts, because the history of philosophy, especially the history since Locke and Descartes, is on the whole in favor of the major contentions of idealism.

Just what should be the method of historical investigation in the hands of idealists? Neo-realists have called for a separation of philosophical research from the study of the history of philosophy, although the very first section of *The New Realism* is an account of " The Historical Significance " of their system, which obviously violates

their own dictum.[5] It seems to me that this is positively
a vicious demand which, if yielded to, would ultimately
result in turning historical studies into dry bones and
research into a sort of disciplined immaturity. If philosophical insight is the goal, it is imperative that philosophical research and the study of the history of philosophy be not separated. With all his *a priori* manufacture
of the course of history, Hegel was the founder of the
history of philosophy; and without some sort of philosophical theory as guiding thread no reading of the history will result in other than a mystic maze. It would
appear to me, then, that idealists should study the history
both in order to develop an idealistic philosophy of history
and also as a means of testing and interpreting the historical systems and idealism itself. Here is a set of tasks
almost inexhaustible and full of rich reward to whoever
will undertake them.[6]

Secondly, there is need of systematic construction.
Here the tasks are more numerous and more baffling than
in the historical field. I shall pick out five specific types
of construction that are perhaps most needed: namely,
an idealistic psychology,[7] a logic, a new facing of the
epistemological problem, a fresh treatment of the relations of science and philosophy today, and last, and perhaps most important, an idealistic philosophy of value.
The very forbidding character of this list elicits one comment at the start: the solving of these problems is obviously the work of a school. The times of encyclopædic
scholarship have passed once for all. The Aristotles and

the Leibniz's and the Herbert Spencers no longer flourish; in fact, Spencer himself was the decay of the type. Scholarship must be largely a credit transaction; no one individual can be an authority in all fields, or in many fields. That this is a limitation is perfectly evident when we consider the narrowness which results in the interests of a great philosopher like John Dewey who, with a remarkable amount of learning, has often been restricted in his thinking by the dictates of his biological approach. While no one can reasonably be censured for not being a Dr. Pangloss, learned in everything, it behooves every specialist to become as broadly acquainted with the work of other specialists in every field as is possible. The need of a genuinely philosophical attitude, the point of view of interest in and respect for every genuine interest of the human spirit, never was so great as it is in these days when no one individual can possibly be acquainted at first hand and thoroughly with any considerable number of those interests. Therefore if intellectual work is to be done on a wide range of difficult problems, it cannot, under the conditions of modern knowledge, be adequately done by any one individual. It is obviously the task of a school. The neo-realists, the critical realists under Drake, Streeter's group in England, all show this philosophical tendency. I am not at all sure that cooperative volumes are the only way, or even the best way, for a school to work. But any frank envisaging of the situation will convince one that cooperative specialization is the need of the hour in philosophy; not for idealism alone, but for every system in that "strife of systems" that seems destined to continue for some time.

Let us turn now, in order, to the five specific types of construction that are particularly needed in idealistic thinking.

First, an idealistic psychology was mentioned. The time was when psychology tried (doubtless unsuccessfully) to be the logos of the psyche. Today it is a commonplace that there is no psyche; or if there is, that psychology has nothing to do with it. Indeed, the present biological dynasty in psychology has brought things to the pass illustrated in the brilliantly written and suggestive work *Psychology from the Standpoint of a Behaviorist*, by J. B. Watson. He frankly admits that he does not know what consciousness means — as indeed he could not know, being a behaviorist; and he is somewhat put to it to distinguish psychology from physiology. In the end, however, he decided that " physiology teaches us concerning the functions of the special organs " whereas psychology arises only when "the physiologist puts the separate organs together again, and turns the whole (man) over to us." The psychologist studies "the total situations in the daily life of an individual that shape his action and conduct." The physiologist, then, studies the organs and functions taken separately; while the psychologist studies those same organs and functions in their joint functioning in the life history of the individual and in his adaptation to environment; studies, for instance, " whether man walks before he crawls, the age at which walking begins, whether walking begins earlier in boys than in girls," and the like. It is to be emphasized that consciousness is not one of the functions in question. What has been called the method of introspection is behaviorized into "verbal report methods," while thinking becomes "subvocal talking." [8]

That is to say, the most modern psychology reduces itself to the study of matter moving in space. It is different from the old materialism that identified consciousness with brain states or their effects but it is nevertheless materialism, and for it the unity of personality, all identity and meaning, all aspiration and value, all reasoning, and all emotion alike are at bottom certain motions of matter. The old faculty psychology was bad; the old rational psychology flew often in the face of facts, not knowing the facts well enough to know that it was flying; but if this behaviorism were offered as an account of consciousness, and not as the purely biological science that it is, it would be just as bad, just as far from the facts, as was the psychology of a hundred years ago. What saves it from this condemnation, and also from being psychology at all, is its frank avowal that it has no concern with consciousness. It is true that not all psychology today is behavioristic; but the behaviorists have cast such a spell over almost everyone else that other psychologists feel that a compromise is necessary. The outcome is an eclectic psychology, which urbanely announces that it is a science of consciousness, but really is for the most part physiology or neurology; or calls itself a science of behavior, but deals with consciousness as usual. Psychology has split. What is called psychology today is largely physiological or experimental (in some physical sense); and such study of consciousness as exists is carried on almost entirely by philosophers or by psychologists with a philosophical interest. But this is unsatisfactory. If personality exists, if there is consciousness, there ought to be a science of them, as well as a metaphysics of personality and a biology of the human animal.

There should be a revival of psychology; not a resuscitation of some old system or text, but a new life in the field. A general psychology of the sort that I have in mind would do justice to the facts of neural basis and function, although emphasizing, as almost no psychology has yet done,[9] the fact that these data belong to a biological propædeutic to psychology and not to psychology itself. The teaching of facts about the sense organs, etc., should be done, both in classroom and in textbooks, by biologists. Psychologists should try to teach what consciousness is, what its own laws and characteristics are, and in particular, the nature and function of the higher conscious activities and of selfhood. Most of the psychological work in this direction seems to be in the hands of men interested in religious education and psychology of religion, who are driven to it by the nature of the subject matter with which they deal. Other educators seem largely to be satisfied with using psychology as a sort of efficiency machine for producing ends more or less naïvely assumed. It should not be supposed that an idealistic psychology would prove a panacea for all our ills, and would serve as a substitute for ethics, metaphysics, and theory of value; by no means. It would, however, serve as an ally instead of as a neutral or an enemy in the war of ideas.

Secondly, work is needed in the field of logic. Logic appears to many to be a barren waste; but, as Daniel Webster once said of Dartmouth College, " There are those that love it." One's logic, in the broad sense, is perhaps the most important thing about one's philosophy. The study of philosophy always requires great intellectual patience; logic may try the patience of the saints beyond endurance. But glance at the history. Socrates was an expert in logical method. Aristotle's greatest contributions were closely connected with his discovery of logic. Kant's Critiques are studies in advanced logic. Hegel's logic is the backbone of his system, and Lotze's of his. Bradley and Bosanquet have each built up their impressive systems on the foundation of a logic. But the great work of past idealists has not settled all logical problems. Never has logical theory been more hotly debated than at the present time. If idealism is on the right track it must avoid the pitfalls of the current types of logic. In particular, it must avoid the fallacies of the organic theory of internal relations advocated by certain idealists; the one-sided and incomplete mathematical-relational analytic logic of neo-realism; and the irrationalism of pragmatism. To develop a distinctively idealistic logic and theory of truth is a task calling for devoted and thorough scholarship and for a vision of the larger implications of the task that not all logicians have possessed. Until this task is accomplished by someone the idealistic organon will be incomplete.

Thirdly, it is essential to develop epistemology in the light of recent discussion and research. The past decade has seen a most extraordinary confusion regarding theory of knowledge. Its importance and its very *Existenz- berechtigung* have been challenged or denied. On the other hand, epistemological problems have stood in the foreground of most debates. D. C. Macintosh's volume on *The Problem of Knowledge* (1915) [10] bears testimony to the lively interest in the field in recent times, as does W. P. Montague's *The Ways of Knowing* (1925).[11]

If I now mention a few epistemological problems that need attention, they are not meant to be taken as the most important or the most vital to idealism but only as samples of what should be done. The doctrine of the categories, for instance, fundamental as it is, has been rendered increasingly obscure by recent work. In particular, investigation should be made of the effect on the theory of the categories of the mathematical analyses of space and time which the neo-realists have exploited. Possibly the most important recent work furnishing materials for this study is N. K. Smith's *Commentary to Kant's Critique of Pure Reason* (1918).[12]

It is also desirable to investigate from the point of view of its relation to idealism the general problem of mediate and immediate knowledge. Recent philosophy puts it in a prominent place. Bergson's doctrine of intuition, Russell's distinction between knowledge by acquaintance and knowledge by description, and Marvin's theory of perception which he uses as a basis for his neo-realistic epistemology, are straws which show which way the wind is blowing. The theories of Bergson and of Russell in particular have been very widely discussed. Absolute and pluralistic personal idealists differ radically at this point.[13] The question at issue is closely related to that of form and content, than which no logical-epistemological question is more complex; it also has bearings not only on our theory of sense experience but also on our interpretation of religious experiences, such as those of the mystics. The question is also related to the whole matter of the activity of the self in knowledge, to which we shall now turn for a moment.

Further, as just implied, it is imperative to study the epistemological significance of the activity of the self in knowledge. Is the self active in immediate knowledge or intuition, if such there be? Is its presence relevant to the epistemological situation in general? The idealist must face the difficulties raised by Perry's essay on " The Ego-Centric Predicament," [14] although the idealist's task is made easier for him by the fact that the ego about which Perry is talking is the biological organism. Idealists may well admit to him that the presence of such an ego is indeed a predicament irrelevant to the knowledge situation and that it should be ignored by one who wishes to understand just what knowledge is. But that the conscious person, the self or subject, may also be ignored with equal impunity, no idealist can admit. On the other hand, that the status of personality is unambiguous and secure in the light of modern psychology (such as it is), epistemology, and metaphysics, scarcely anyone but an idealist will admit. There is still much work to do in this field; many problems await solution, others even formulation.

Fourthly, brief mention should be made of the great need of working out a better understanding of the relations between science and philosophy. The conceptions of science have broadened very rapidly of late and there are always new questions arising in this field. It can hardly be said that Ward's *Naturalism and Agnosticism,* with its numerous new editions, has brought the problem up to date. I mention this problem, not to discuss it, but to call attention to the need of an *entente cordiale* with the sciences which shall not result in the surrender of philosophy to science, and to the corresponding need of some men, trained in the natural sciences, who shall devote themselves to philosophical problems.

Fifthly, there is need for an idealistic theory of values. The value-problem has been studied from every angle in the past twenty-five or thirty years — its psychological, ethical, religious, metaphysical, and applied aspects. But it is not far from the truth to say that the net yield has been disappointing. Of all the problems of philosophy none is closer to the heart of life than this; indeed it is the very problem of the heart of life. If philosophy is to justify itself as an interpretation of life, the theory of value ought to furnish results of the most illuminating and practical significance for the understanding and the guidance of human civilization. If progress is possible in philosophy at all, it ought to be possible in the theory of values. Nevertheless, as aforesaid, although value-theory has been intensively cultivated of late, it has yielded relatively little practical insight; he would be daring who asserted that modern thought has advanced much beyond Plato in this respect. It seems to me that the most valuable contribution that has been made is that in Sorley's *Moral Values and the Idea of God* which is the most satisfactory argument for the objectivity of moral values and the dependence of all value upon personality that I have seen. But it suffers from what James would call thinness, that is, a certain lack of sufficient contact with actual experience. Philosophy, and all thinking, must be in some sense abstract. A reasoned account of life can never be illustrated by photographs of the thoughts. But philosophy, and particularly theory of value, has as sole function the interpretation and criticism of experience and cannot swing in the air. If the questions of value-theory could be answered, it would make a real difference in life. Some of these questions are: What are the supreme values of life? On what basis ought we to decide that one value is more valuable than another? Are there different types of criteria for different kinds of value? Is there an essential unity in the whole life of value? Is value objective or subjective? Is it essentially an experience of personality or not? Here ethical, logical, esthetic, metaphysical, epistemological, and practical considerations meet.   If idealists can do something more toward interpreting and clarifying the data of value experience, they will perform a real intellectual service.   If any philosophical school ought to do this effectively, it is precisely the idealistic.   The efforts of realists in the field — G. E. Moore, S. Alexander, Perry, and Spaulding, for example — have led to such diverse and contradictory results that one can scarcely hope for any really unified and fruitful realistic theory of value.   On the other hand, recent idealism justifies the hope that if a superstructure be erected on the foundations of idealistic theory it will prove to retain the inward coherence of absolutism, while surpassing both speculative philosophy and neo-realism in contacts with real experience.

Let us now turn to the next general type of task awaiting idealists.   It is what I have called practical construction.   The use of such a term demands an explanation in this connection.   It seems to imply that the long preceding discussion of systematic construction dealt with the purely theoretical and hence impractical; whereas now we are to leave system and theory behind in the pursuit of the truly practical.   This implication not only is not intended but even seems to me to misrepresent the truth. I regard the distinction of the theoretical and practical as one of the most misunderstood and misleading of abstractions.   All life is activity, is practice; all reality is alive, everything flows, except the abiding self — and one of the most prominent traits of the abiding self is its activity!

All theory, if it be valid, is an account of this activity and is itself an activity; that is, theory is an activity that interprets activity. On the other hand, all practical life is, if it be not utterly blind *empirisches Herumtappen,* as Kant once said, an expression of theory, guided by theory, loyal to theory. The separation between theory and practice is a distinction that a single mind makes in dealing with different aspects of a reality that is essentially one. There are good practice and bad practice, which embody good theory and bad theory. But all judgment of practice as good or bad is a matter of theory. There is no conflict between theory and practice in essence, but only a conflict among theories. Some, indeed, do not accept this view of the case. Durant Drake, chairman of the critical realists, has said that metaphysics and epistemology inhabit a realm utterly apart from life. He thinks that they are indeed interesting intellectual exercises but that they have no bearing on conduct. Far be it from me to deny that such abstract intellectual exercise is possible; if doubted, this would be sufficiently proved by the achievements of "logistic," with its universes of discourse that have nothing to do with our universe. Between Bertrand Russell's mathematics and our real world there is a great gulf fixed. These instances of pure theory would fill the man on the street, spoiling for a fight with theory, full of mingled delight and rage. But after all, the man on the street would be fighting a man of straw. True *theoria* is indeed an intellectual contemplation; but it is a contemplation of principles that relate to, explain, interpret, and criticize our actual human life. All philosophy worth having is philosophy of life and hence is a search for the meaning of actual experiences taken as a whole.

And so, when I talk about practical construction, I am really talking only about that part of theory which has its applications in some of the more obvious and visible phases of human life. I shall mention only three of these phases which ought to be of special interest to idealists, namely, the social, the educational, and the religious.

The need of socially progressive idealism has already been mentioned. The social problem is the chief practical problem of our time. Its urgency is pressed on us in every daily paper, in every purchase, in every contact with our fellows. The utmost intellectual resources of humanity are being taxed, and will be taxed for a long time to come, in coping with the complex phenomena. To whom should we look for light in solving the problems? To the economists? Assuredly. To the labor leaders? It would be folly to neglect them. To the capitalists? To them too. To the sociologists and historians and political scientists? Yes, to all of these and to the specialists in every science. But all the wisdom of these wise men is folly if they leave neglected the question as to the meaning and worth of human life, and the goal for which men ought to strive. A true social philosophy must put ethics in the foreground manifestly, if it is to be true to the best in human nature. And an idealist, anyway, would add not ethics only, but metaphysics. For idealism, the whole problem of reality is a social problem; and every conflict in human relations involves our relations to that "great *socius*" whom religion calls God. Our conception of what social relations ought to be must be affected both by our theory of value and by our metaphysics, and hence, manifestly, by our religion.

No social movement can long survive among civilized men which does not produce a philosophy that satisfies at least its own members. Philosophy both causes and reflects practical programs. Sometimes these programs are not carried out, as in Plato's case; yet even Utopias inspire actual social changes. Is not the Kingdom of God itself a Utopia? But often a political theory or an economic theory growing out of epistemological and metaphysical as well as ethical reflection shapes the actual course of events far more than the actors in the events realized. Locke, Rousseau, and the French Revolution. Hegel and *der Staat* which was the kingdom of God. . . . Hegel again and Marx and Engels. . . . Marx and Tolstoi and Russia today. We should, indeed, beware of being ideologists; ideas alone do not cause great social and historical changes. But without the part played by philosophers the course of history would have been radically different from what it has been. I am concerned at present only to show that idealistic philosophy has in the present crisis a golden opportunity; and that, in order to meet it, it should not abdicate but rather reassert its function as philosophy.

Another practical matter to which I had referred is the

educational problem. This is part of the general social problem, and, I am inclined to think, the most important part of it. Until there is general education, the masses cannot understand their own situation or seek intelligently to improve it; and until there is a widespread and adequate moral and religious education, intelligence will be directed, as at present, to selfish and unworthy ends. It is evident that the great need of the hour is for an educational philosophy based on a sound theory of values. Here again is an opportunity for idealists that is of the utmost importance. The difficulties with current education are ultimately traceable to the lack of genuine idealism in the community. Again, let me say, we should not imagine that a philosophical system can solve the whole problem or that the correct theory of educational values will produce a race of uniformly good specimens of the *genus homo;* but granting the fallacy of ideology once more, we may venture the belief that a sound understanding of the meaning and values of life in the light of an idealistic philosophy might go farther than we dream toward revolutionizing society.

The third practical matter is the religious. Every problem is infinite, that of religion most obviously so. Although some might be tempted to say that Bowne's work in theism, for example, is pretty nearly definitive, reflection would guard us against such a conclusion. The problem is too complex and many-sided; too much new work is being done by the historians and psychologists; too many new conditions in life are arising and too many new infants are being born annually to permit us ever to regard the discussion as closed.   The adaptability of idealism for interpreting the religious basis of civilization, of life, and of thought is too obvious to need further amplification in a discussion which is concerned only with pointing out tasks.

Finally, the need of self-criticism, *auto-critique,* should be emphasized.   Whatever our philosophical interests or convictions, they are more apt to be fruitful and cogent if we frequently entertain the ideal of the possibility of improving them.   Conviction without dogmatism or, if you please, dogmatism [15] without a sense of personal infallibility is essential to philosophical development. While we should not always be pulling the plant up by the roots to see if it is growing; and while certain fundamental points of view in the attitude of any thinker may remain unchanged throughout his intellectual career; it is nevertheless true that an occasional reexamination of first principles is necessary to prevent smug complacency and philosophical stagnation.

IV

If this book has had a single aim, it has been to show that ideals are fundamental to mind, to nature, and to society.   But man's knowledge of true ideals is always growing; and new ideals are always being shaped.   Ideals, then, form no fixed and completed system.   It may be granted that idealism aims to be a system and some of its principles may, indeed, be " fixed."   But, in the larger sense, idealism is not fixed. It is itself an ideal. It is a constant reinterpretation of the individual and of society and of their environment. Its aim is both a discovery of the truth about the structure of reality and also a creation of new values within the limits imposed by the nature of things. Its appeal is neither to convention nor to authority; yet it sees the futility of mere blind experimentation which " tries anything once," irrespective of truth or past experience. It appeals to the ideal of reason – that is, to the living unity of experience apprehended as a related whole, insofar as the human mind is capable of such apprehension. I say " the ideal of reason " for, of course, reason is an " ought-to-be-yet-cannot-be " ideal. The true idealist is therefore the most sophisticated realist. He has considered experience as a whole, yet is fully aware that there is always more to learn. He is less likely to be taken by surprise than anyone who has failed to seek the unified view of reason. But, as long as we live in a growing universe, it is impossible that the work of idealism will ever be completed.

NOTES

CHAPTER I

1. J. M. Guyau, *A Sketch of Morality Independent of Obligation or Sanction* (London: Watts, 1898), p. 38, etc. The original title is *Esquisse d'une morale sans obligation ni sanction* (1885).

2. This assertion is denied by current pragmatism-realism. John Dewey's article, "An Empirical Account of Appearance" in *Jour. Phil.*, 24(1927), 449–463, is an excellnt statement of the point of view which I regard as incorrect. "Appearance," that is, presentation in experience, is, he admits, always "to somebody"; but this does not involve "dependence upon the mind or consciousness in or to which a thing appears" (p. 450). Over against this, it seems to me that the appearance is nothing but consciousness. It is true that the thing which "appears" may be independent of the consciousness to which it appears; but the appearance is purely and wholly conscious awareness or apprehension. Dewey says that "a presentation marks the existence of a thing in relation to an organism" (p. 451). It may "mark" it, if it is not an illusion or an hallucination; but "marking" means *presenting to consciousness* (Dewey says "convey into view," p. 461), and this is not identical with the existence of the thing, unless one is prepared to be a literal Berkeleian minus Berkeley's God.

3. Madison Bentley and others, *Psychologies of 1925* (Worcester, Massachusetts: Clark University, 1926).

4. Jared Sparks Moore, *The Foundations of Psychology* (Princeton: Princeton University Press, 1921).

5. Hans Driesch, *The Crisis in Psychology* (Princeton: Princeton University Press, 1925).

6. Knight Dunlap, "The Use and Abuse of Abstractions in Psychology" in *Phil. Rev.*, 36(1927), 462–487.

7. Typical statements of that point of view are found in Shadworth Hodgson's *Theory of Practice*, 2 Vols. (London: Longmans, 1870). *Cf.* Vol. I, pp. 338–339, 416. " Pain must be held to be no warning to abstain from the thing which has caused pain; pleasure no motive to seek the thing which has caused pleasure; pain no check, pleasure no spur to action." Consciousness when it arises is "not a new existence but the perception of the pre-existing world," "nothing but a mirror or reduplication of the pre-existing and simultaneously existing world" (*ibid.*).

8. The standard English edition is R. D. Hicks, *Aristotle: De Anima* (Cambridge, England: University Press, 1907).

9. For an excellent presentation of the purposive point of view, see William McDougall, *Outline of Psychology* (N. Y.: Scribner, 1923).

10. *Proceedings of the Sixth International Congress of Philosophy* (N. Y.: Longmans, 1927), p. 25. This work will hereafter be referred to as *Proceedings Sixth Congress*.

11. The formula in the text was independently arrived at. Since Chapter I was written, my attention has been drawn to C. A. Strong's thesis that in introspection "the self is not only the true but the sole datum," *The Origin of Consciousness* (London: Macmillan, 1918), p. 105. But for Strong the self is datum in introspection only; yet not in introspection only but in all experience is the self the datum. — The importance of the problem of the datum is well stated by R. W. Sellars, who says, "I do not think that my statement is too strong when I assert that the refusal to distinguish between datum and object is at the foundation of all the vagaries of modern philosophy," *Evolutionary Naturalism* (Chicago: Open Court, 1922), p. 27. Writers so different as Bergson (in his *Essai sur les données immédiates de la conscience*, "Essay on the immediate data of consciousness," — unhappily translated as *Time and Free Will*) and Husserl (whose phenomenology is based on antipsychologism) are

essentially concerned with the problem of the self as datum. The view has obvious relations to the thought of Augustine, Descartes, Schopenhauer, and many others.

12. The neo-realists and neo-scholastics both hold that " a datum need not be exclusively either internal or external, but may at one and the same time be both," James H. Ryan, " Does Natural Realism Break Down? " *The New Scholasticism*, 1(1927), 256. This view implies the identity of idea and object — epistemological monism — which I have criticized in my *An Introduction to Philosophy* (N. Y.: Holt, 1925), Chap. III. *Cf.* also, note 2 above.

13. G. Dawes Hicks, " Sensible Appearances and Material Things " (*Proceedings Sixth Congress*, pp. 224–236), where several views of the datum are discussed and criticized. The passage in the text is on p. 228. For a clear and logical criticism of the neo-realistic view of essences see A. W. Moore's paper, " Subsistence and Existence in Neo-Realism " (*ibid.*, pp. 278–284).

14. William James, *Psychology* (N. Y.: Holt, 1890 and later editions), Vol. II, p. 3.

15. See C. A. Strong, " On the Nature of the Datum " in D. Drake and others, *Studies in Critical Realism* (London: Macmillan, 1920), pp. 223–244 and also the other essays in that volume. See also D. Drake, *Mind and Its Place in Nature* (N. Y.: Macmillan, 1925), pp. 7–8 *et passim*. George Boas has written an excellent criticism of this view in an article on " The Datum as Essence " in *Jour. Phil.*, 24(1927), 487–497. — The pragmatic view of what is immediately given is well worked out in Joseph K. Hart, *Inside Experience* (N. Y.: Longmans, 1927).

16. J. Loewenberg, " Pre-Analytical and Post-Analytical Data," *Jour. Phil.*, 24(1927), 5–14.

17. Aristotle, *De Anima* II, 6 (p. 77); see note 8 above. See also Descartes: " But it will be said that these presentations are false, and that I am dreaming. Let it be so. At all events it is certain that I seem to see light, hear a noise, and feel heat; this cannot be

false, and this is what in me is properly called perceiving (*sentire*), which is nothing else than thinking," Meditation II, from Veitch's tr., *The Meditations and Selections from the Principles of René Descartes* (Chicago: Open Court, 1913), p. 35.

18. This distinction is the same as that made by John Grote between what he calls " self-self " (the datum) and " thought-self " in *Exploratio Philosophica* (Cambridge, England: University Press, 1900), pp. 145–147.

19. Compare J. Royce, *The Problem of Christianity* (N. Y.: Macmillan, 1913), Vol. II, p. 61. "However a man may come by his ideal of himself, the self is no mere datum, but is in its essence a life which is interpreted, and which interprets itself, and which, apart from some sort of ideal interpretation, is a mere flight of ideas, or a meaningless flow of feelings, or a vision that sees nothing, or else a barren abstract conception." It seems to me that in this passage Royce disparages the datum unduly; for if the principle of interpretation and of selfhood is not somehow in the very datum, it is hard to see how one can arrive at a view of the whole, save by magic. But Royce is quite right in his insistence that thought must move from the datum to the whole.

20. Cited by Bruno Bauch, *Die Idee* (Leipzig: Reinicke, 1926), p. 257.

21. See Philip E. Wheelwright, "The Category of Self-Transcendence," *Proceedings Sixth Congress*, pp. 121–128.

22. The critical realist, Durant Drake, would go further than the position indicated in the text. In *Studies in Critical Realism* (see note 15 above), he holds that " our instinctive (and practically inevitable) belief in the existence of the physical world about us is pragmatically justifiable," although we cannot " deduce " any " proof " of existence. This pragmatic justification, based on an implied distinction between pragmatic basis and rational proof, seems to me to make that distinction much too sharp. Yet what Drake means by pragmatic working and what I mean by rational hypothesis point in the same direction, although I lay more stress than he

seems to lay on the rational character of the " pragmatic " hypothesis. George Boas (in the article quoted in note 15) objects, as I do, to a " non-logical act of faith " (p. 497) but well says that " the suppression of all hypothesis or postulates in thinking would not open the way for 'instinct,' but for silence " (p. 492). R. W. Nelson has worked out interesting suggestions on the hypothetical (or experimental) nature of thought. See his " Fundamentalism and Experimental Logic " in the *American Review* (September–October, 1925), reprinted in November, 1925 as Vol. XI, No. 10, of *The Culver-Stockton College Bulletin* (Canton, Missouri), and other articles.

23. D. H. Parker, *The Self and Nature* (Cambridge: Harvard University Press, 1917), p. 143.

24. For a treatment of certain creative aspects of mental activity, see E. S. Brightman, *Religious Values* (N. Y.: Abingdon Press, 1925), Chap. IX, " Worship as Creativity."

25. G. A. Wilson, *The Self and Its World* (N. Y.: Macmillan, 1926), is an admirable exposition of the view of things which grows out of explaining the stimuli to which the self responds as metaphysical rather than biological. See also R. T. Flewelling's thoughtful study, *Creative Personality* (N. Y.: Macmillan, 1926).

26. G. A. Coe, *Psychology of Religion* (Chicago: University of Chicago Press, 1916), pp. 32–42. The entire passage should be read with care.

27. W. E. Hocking, " Mind and Near-Mind " in *Proceedings Sixth Congress,* p. 214.

CHAPTER II

1. Durant Drake, *Mind and Its Place in Nature* (N. Y.: Macmillan, 1925), p. 78.

2. A. N. Whitehead, *Science and the Modern World,* 1st ed. (N. Y.: Macmillan, 1925), p. 211. But Whitehead's alternative view is hardly enlightening. He says that " the private psychological field

is merely the event considered from its own standpoint" (*ibid.*, p. 209). Omitting any reference to the technical definition of "event" (see *ibid.*, pp. 102, 168, etc.), it appears that Whitehead's statement ignores the difference between an "event" and the act of "considering it from its own standpoint." One of two things seems to be true: either the event is itself a thinker, capable of "considering," or else some self, not identical with the event, "considers" the event. In either case, a datum-self is needed, for even in the former case the act of considering cannot be the same aspect of the event as that which is "considered."

3. A. S. Pringle-Pattison, *The Idea of God in Recent Philosophy* (N. Y.: Oxford University Press, 1917), p. 110, etc.

4. John Locke, *An Essay Concerning Human Understanding* III, vi, 9.

5. See S. Radhakrishnan, "The Doctrine of Māyā: Some Problems" in *Proceedings Sixth Congress*, pp. 683–689.

6. "Für Aristoteles und für die Griechen überhaupt die scharfe Trennung zwischen Seele and Leib, wie in der modernen Seelenlehre, besteht nicht." Note by J. H. v. Kirchmann on Aristotle, *De Anima* (Leipzig: Dürr, 1871), A, IV, p. 36.

7. *Encyclopædia Britannica*, Vol. 17, p. 232b.

8. A. N. Whitehead, *op. cit.*, p. 206.

9. P. W. Bridgman, *The Logic of Modern Physics* (N. Y.: Macmillan, 1927), p. vii. Yet see the admirable work of E. W. Hobson, *The Domain of Natural Science* (N. Y.: Macmillan, 1923).

10. Max Planck, *A Survey of Physics* (N. Y.: Dutton, 1925), p. 5.

11. Ernst Cassirer, *Substance and Function and Einstein's Theory of Relativity* (Chicago: Open Court, 1923), pp. 129–130.

12. *Ibid.*, p. 141.

13. Victor E. Levine, "Spiritual Values in Science" in *The Scientific Monthly*, 25(1927), 119–126. The passage quoted is on p. 119.

14. G. A. Wilson, *The Self and Its World* (N. Y.: Macmillan, 1926).

15. L. T. Troland, *The Mystery of Mind* (N. Y.: Van Nostrand, 1926), p. 44.

16. *Ibid.*, p. 60.

17. E. A. Burtt, *The Metaphysical Foundations of Modern Physical Science* (N. Y.: Harcourt, 1925), p. 327. A similar idea was expressed by W. W. Campbell: "A scientist does not create the truth. He does nothing whatever to the truth; he simply uncovers it" (cited by D. H. Menzel, *Science*, 65(1927), 431, May 6, 1927). Do not such utterances inspire in some readers a wonder how scientists can do so much while doing so little? — a curiosity as to how the truth about electrons is "uncovered" without any creative activity by the scientist?

18. A. N. Whitehead, *op. cit.*, p. 202.

19. Durant Drake, *op. cit.*, Chaps. VII and VIII, esp. pp. 91, 97, and 99.

20. P. W. Bridgman, *op. cit.*, p. xi.

21. *Ibid.*, pp. viii, 54.

22. *Ibid.*, p. 5 *et passim*.

23. *Ibid.*, p. 6. Equally positivistic is the following quotation: "No operations of measuring motion have been found to be useful in describing simply the behavior of nature which are not operations relative to a single observer," *ibid.*, p. 27. It may also be added that Einstein inclines to view the presuppositions of physics as "mere conventions, like the order of words in a dictionary." *Cit.*, Hugo Dingler, *Der Zusammenbruch der Wissenschaft* (Munich: Reinhardt, 1926), p. 72, note. See also Henri Poincaré.

24. *Cf.* G. T. W. Patrick's interesting article, "The Convergence of Evolution and Fundamentalism" in *The Scientific Monthly,* 23(1926), 5–15. *Cf.* also the papers on emergence in *Proceedings Sixth Congress,* and the posthumously published paper by Alfred H. Lloyd, "Also the Emergence of Matter," *Jour. Phil.,* 24(1927), 309–332.

25. Max Planck, *op. cit.,* pp. 42–70, and esp. p. 51.

26. P. W. Bridgman, *op. cit.,* p. 47.

27. Ralph S. Lillie, "Physical Indeterminism and Vital Action" in *Science,* 66(1927), 139–144.

28. Claude Bernard, *Experimental Medicine* (N. Y.: Macmillan, 1927), cited by Lillie in *Science,* 66(1927), 143.

29. Whitehead, *op. cit., passim,* argues for an organic view as opposed to the mechanistic.

30. Ralph Barton Perry, *The Present Conflict of Ideals* (N. Y.: Longmans, 1918), Chap. V, pp. 45–62.

31. C. E. Ayres, *Science: the False Messiah* (Indianapolis: Bobbs-Merrill, 1927).

32. Arthur Lynch, *Science: Leading and Misleading.* (N. Y.: Dutton, 1927).

33. Hugo Dingler, *op. cit.*

34. Bridgman says: "All the discussion of this essay has been subject to one explicit assumption, namely, that the working of our minds is understood, which of course involves the assumption that our minds continue to function in the future in the same way as in the past," *op. cit.,* p. 197.

35. Note also, "But it is a question whether . . . any picture that we can form of nature will not be tinged — sicklied o'er with the pale cast of thought," *ibid.,* p. 94, and also, "It is precisely here, in an improved understanding of our mental relations to nature,

that the permanent contribution of relativity is to be found," *ibid.*, p. 2. Especially relevant to the incident in the text is the following remark of Cassirer's: " The naïve view, that measurements inhere in physical things and processes like sensuous properties, and only need to be read off from them, is more and more superseded with the advance of theoretical physics," *ibid.*, p. 146.

36. *Cf.* A. N. Whitehead, *op. cit., passim.*

37. Cf. E. W. Hobson, *op. cit.*, pp. 454, 455, and 26. See note 9.

38. Hugo Dingler, *op. cit.*, p. 5.

Chapter III

1. See John Dewey's article referred to in Chapter I, note 2. See also R. F. A. Hoernlé, *Studies in Contemporary Metaphysics* (N. Y.: Harcourt, 1920), Chapter V on " Saving the Appearances."

2. Ralph Barton Perry is a realist who recognizes this fact. He says, " If reality be 'the ideal of thought,' as in a sense it undoubtedly is, then it must on realistic grounds be possible to regard this as a rôle which reality assumes without prejudice to its independence." See E. B. Holt and others, *The New Realism* (N. Y.: Macmillan, 1912), p. 117. Ideals must be recognized but must be interpreted in a manner compatible with realism.

3. Oswald Spengler, *Der Untergang des Abendlandes*, 2 Vols., 33d to 47th ed. (Munich: Beck, 1923); also in English tr.

4. M. C. Otto, *Things and Ideals* (N. Y.: Holt, 1924), p. 5.

5. Hugo Dingler, *op. cit.*, p. 142.

6. P. F. Voelker, *The Function of Ideals and Attitudes in Social Education* (N. Y.: Teachers College, Columbia University, 1921), now out of print.

7. For a discussion of the subject, see Goodwin B. Watson, " Character Tests," *Religious Education*, 22(1927), 500–504.

8. See B. Kellermann, *Das Ideal im System der Kantischen Philosophie* (Berlin: Schwetschke, 1920).

9. Ralph Barton Perry, *op. cit.*

10. *Op. cit.*, see note 4.

11. *Ibid.*, pp. 8–9.

12. Article, "Epistemology" in Hastings, *Encyclopædia of Religion and Ethics*, Vol. V, p. 352.

13. For some indication of the empirical confusion that obtains, see the admirable study of motivation in M. K. Thomson, *The Springs of Human Action* (N. Y.: Appleton, 1927).

14. P. F. Voelker, *op. cit.*, p. 47. The definition was formulated by a Committee on Education for Citizenship, appointed by Dean James E. Russell from the faculty of Teachers College.

15. W. D. Niven, article, "Ideal" in Hastings, *Encyclopædia of Religion and Ethics*, Vol. VII, pp. 86–87.

16. The statement in the text does not imply that emotional attitude toward ideals is unimportant. It is of the utmost importance in practical life and in education. Bagley is quite right, from the practical point of view, when he says: "Ideals dominate large adjustments. Their intellectual content is often simple; the emotional factor is the important one." *Cit.*, Voelker, *op. cit.*, p. 53. Voelker, however, goes too far when he says that "genetically, our ideals emerge when our emotionalized experiences are generalized, that is, when they are raised to the level of an idea" (*ibid.*, p. 40). While this is doubtless true of the dawn of the first idealizing experiences of primitive man, and while E. L. Thorndike is correct in saying that "ideals are kith and kin of man's original hungers and thirsts and cravings," *Educational Psychology* (N. Y.: Teachers College, Columbia University, 1910) Vol. I, pp. 310–312, yet it is erroneous to infer that what was true of the primitive origin of ideals is universally true of their present nature. Some ideals are, it is true, conceptualized emotions; others are emotionalized concepts, and still

others are almost wholly unemotional approvals of a possible experience.   In any event, the presence or absence of the emotion at the origin or in the development of the ideal has nothing to do with the question of whether it would be a good thing (a "value") to realize the ideal in question.

17. H. Schwarz, *Das Ungegebene* (Tübingen: Mohr, 1921).

18. G. W. Cunningham, in *Five Lectures on the Problem of Mind* (Austin: University of Texas Press, 1925), pp. 98–99, speaks of "ideal schemes," "systems," and "structures," as synonymous.

19. Despite the importance of the activity and process for ideals, that aspect may be exaggerated.   E. C. Lindeman, for instance, has said that "activities are to be evaluated, not in terms of their rational ends, but rather in terms of activities themselves.   No end is to be held sufficiently worthy to justify a means; ends are to be invested with integrity only as they are justified by adequate and rational means" (*The New Republic,* November 19, 1924).   But it is not apparent how activities are to be evaluated without thinking about the reasonableness of the ideals which they embody or imply. The "rational end" is not the conclusion of the process, the final term in the activity series.   That has been made clear in the text. But the rational end as the meaning of the process itself, the type or pattern which it is working out, must be appealed to if any sort of judgment is to be passed on the activity; that type must, of course, be considered in relation to other possible types and to other actual types in process of realization.

20. See Graham Wallas, *The Great Society* (N. Y.: Macmillan, 1914).   This book, which prophesied the World War just before its outbreak, dwells on the complexity of modern society.

21. Bertrand Russell, *What I Believe* (N. Y.: Dutton, 1925), a work of brilliant confusion, defines the good life most beautifully as one "inspired by love and guided by knowledge" (p. 20).   The emphasis on love in relation to ideals goes back, of course, to Plato. In recent thought it is made central by Franz Brentano, in *Vom Ursprung sittlicher Erkenntnis,* 2nd ed. (Leipzig: Meiner, 1921),

translated by Cecil Hague as *The Origin of the Knowledge of Right and Wrong* (Westminster: Constable, 1902). See paragraph 27, especially.

22. C. D. Burns, *The Contact Between Minds* (London: Macmillan, 1923), p. 3.

23. Kant traced the Primacy of the Practical Reason back to Plato. " Plato fand seine Ideen vorzüglich in allem was praktisch ist, d.i. auf Freiheit beruht " (Plato found his Ideas chiefly in everything that is practical, *i.e.*, rests on freedom). Kant, *Kritik der reinen Vernunft*, A314, B371.

24. Ernst Cassirer, *op. cit.*, p. 144.

25. Max Planck, *op. cit.*, pp. 22, 41.

26. See Chapter I of this book.

27. Moritz Geiger, " Oberflächen- und Tiefenwirkung der Kunst " in *Proceedings Sixth Congress,* pp. 462–468.

28. This is the substance of the famous " ontological argument " for the being of God.

29. Substantially this view, although with qualifications, is supported in B. Russell's *What I Believe,* already referred to. Contrast this with Rufus M. Jones, *The Fundamental Ends of Life* (N. Y.: Macmillan, 1924)! Compare Kant's definition of " wisdom " as " the Idea of the necessary unity of all possible ends " (*Kritik der reinen Vernunft*, A328, B385).

30. See A. C. Knudson, *The Philosophy of Personalism* (N. Y.: Abingdon, 1925), pp. 148–152, 224–225.

31. For a more detailed study of the meaning of " ought " and " obligation " for ethics see E. S. Brightman, *Religious Values* (N. Y.: Abingdon, 1927), pp. 32–69. For one of the most famous attacks on the validity of obligation see J. M. Guyau, *A Sketch of Morality Independent of Obligation or Sanction* (London: Watts, 1898).

32. See W. Windelband, *Präludien*, 9th ed. (Tübingen: Mohr, 1924), especially the essay "Normen und Naturgesetze" (Vol. II, pp. 59–98), and *Einleitung in die Philosophie*, 2nd ed. (Tübingen: Mohr, 1920), which has been translated into English by Joseph McCabe as *Introduction to Philosophy* (N. Y.: Oxford University Press, 1922). Maurice Picard in *Values: Immediate and Contributory* (N. Y.: New York University Press, 1920) has rightly pointed out that in the essay in *Präludien* just mentioned, norms "appear as a selection from a manifold of possible — and actual — experiences," while in the essay on Immanuel Kant "they are the conditions of any possible experience at all" (p. 130). The latter view (taking "possible experience" to mean coherent and thinkable experience) is that of Kant and is, in principle, the one held by the present writer and defended in the text.

33. R. W. Sellars, *Evolutionary Naturalism* (Chicago: Open Court, 1922) gives one of the simplest and clearest recent accounts of naturalism by a man genuinely concerned about the ideals of human living. S. Alexander, *Space, Time, and Deity* (London: Macmillan, 1920) is naturalism in the grand style, yet so liberal and truly philosophical in spirit that it is almost as idealistic as naturalistic.

34. The term "objective structure" is used and discussed at length by G. P. Adams in *Idealism and the Modern Age* (N. H.: Yale University Press, 1919).

35. Robert Shafer, *Christianity and Naturalism* (N. H.: Yale University Press, 1926) is concerned with essentially the same problem as is confronted in the text. See a review of Shafer by the present writer in *The Philosophical Review*, September, 1927. See also E. S. Brightman, *An Introduction to Philosophy* (N. Y.: Holt, 1925), Chap. VII, "The Chief Philosophical World Views."

36. Robert Shafer, *op. cit.*, p. 289.

37. Hegel, *Encyclopädie* edited by G. Lasson (Leipzig: Meiner, 1920), section 6, p. 37. Tr. by the present writer.

38. The hypothesis suggested in the text was arrived at independently, largely as a result of reflection on the facts of evolution

and on considerations suggested by E. Noble in *Purposive Evolution* (N. Y.: Holt, 1926). However, I owe to R. M. Vaughan a reference to a passage in J. H. Snowden, *The World a Spiritual System* (N. Y.: Macmillan, 1910), which reads as follows: "Does this mean that this stress [of nature] enters into the life of God as a personal experience? The suggestion is highly speculative, but the tendency is strong to think that it may contain some deep and mysterious truth . . ." pp. 267–268.

CHAPTER IV

1. This is Russell's view.

2. B. Russell, *What I Believe* (previously quoted), p. 59.

3. *The Saturday Review of Literature*, April 4, 1925, editorial page.

4. *Science*, 65(1927), 259.

5. Editorial, "Concerning Gods" in *The Saturday Review of Literature*, October 25, 1924.

6. In discussion at the 1925 meeting of the American Philosophical Association (Eastern Division).

7. *Journal of the Barnes Foundation*, January, 1926, p. 14.

8. Note the other discussions of science in this book. See Index.

9. P. W. Bridgman, *The Logic of Modern Physics*, p. 143.

10. "To be liberal a college must be essentially intellectual." A. Meiklejohn, *The Liberal College* (Boston: Marshall Jones Company, 1920), p. 30.

11. John Locke, *An Essay Concerning Human Understanding*, IV, xix, 4.

12. See John Dewey, *Reconstruction in Philosophy* (N. Y.: Holt, 1920), Chap. I, where the view described in the text is defended.

13. In *Science,* April 15, 1927. An opposing point of view, akin to that of the present writer, is expressed by J. S. Moore in an article, "Philosophy and the Sciences" in *Science,* September 16, 1927.

14. The famous passage reads, "Our ultimate standard of worth is an ideal of *personal* worth. All other values are relative to value for, of, or in a person." T. H. Green, *Prolegomena to Ethics* (Oxford: Clarendon Press, 1906), p. 210.

15. The reference is, of course, to Nietzsche's doctrine of the Superman, and the distinction between *Herrenmoral* and *Sklavenmoral* (Morals of Lords and Morals of Slaves).

Chapter V

1. See Chapter VI of this book.

2. Quoted at length in the *Boston Evening Transcript* of August 25, 1923, p. 14. Lord Birkenhead was there reported as saying that "the great Bentham long since pointed out that the motive spring, and the necessary motive spring, of human endeavor, was self-interest." He also said that "the world probably would not survive if idealism were given a completely free rein." It is true that he wrongly takes idealism to mean that each individual should "regulate his or her life not upon his or her own interests but upon some supposed interests of others." It is interesting to see revealed here the logical atomism which has always characterized purely individualistic thought. True idealism, however, is not the setting of the interests of others over against one's own; it is rather that view of the total situation which provides adequately for all interests in organic interrelations. This description, I think, applies both to social and to metaphysical idealism as distinguished from social and metaphysical atomism.

3. See H. J. Rogers (editor), *Congress of Arts and Science, Universal Exposition, St. Louis, 1904* (Boston: Houghton Mifflin, 1905), Vol. I, pp. 169–452.

4. See Chapter III of this book.

5. R. F. A. Hoernlé, *Idealism as a Philosophy* (N. Y.: Doran, 1927), p. 316.

6. E. G. Spaulding, *The New Rationalism* (N. Y.: Holt, 1918), pp. vi–vii.

7. M. C. Otto, *op. cit.*, p. 44.

8. C. D. Broad, *The Mind and Its Place in Nature* (N. Y.: Harcourt, 1925), pp. 5–6.

9. From a newspaper clipping, source unknown.

10. B. M. Laing, *A Study in Moral Problems* (London: Allen, 1922), pp. 197–198.

11. *The Scientific Monthly*, September, 1925, p. 292.

12. J. H. Leuba, *Belief in God and Immortality* (Boston: Sherman French, 1916).

13. E. D. Martin, *The Mystery of Religion* (N. Y.: Harper, 1924), p. 120. The state of intelligence in these United States may be judged from the fact that a Christian minister has endorsed this book as the best treatment of mystical religion which he knows.

14. E. D. Martin, *op. cit.*, p. 112.

15. G. B. Watson, "Virtues versus Virtue," *School and Society*, September 3, 1927, pp. 286–290.

16. *Ibid.*, p. 287.

17. Johannes Müller, "Wider den Idealismus," *Die Christliche Welt*, August 18, 1927, Columns 728–745.

18. The quotations from Nietzsche are translations made by the present writer chiefly from passages in *Also Sprach Zarathustra* and selections "Aus dem Nachlass."

19. Of his many writings, perhaps *Scepticism and Animal Faith* (N. Y.: Scribner, 1923) is the most comprehensive.

Chapter VI

1. Royce, *Lectures on Modern Idealism* (N. H.: Yale University Press, 1919), p. 235.

2. M. R. Cohen's articles in *The New Republic* call attention to the importance of these periodicals in the development of American thought.

3. Vol. 1, 1910; Vol. 2, 1911; Vol. 3, 1913.

4. Paul Natorp, *Die logischen Grundlagen der exakten Wissenschaften* (Leipzig: Teubner, 1910).

5. *Mind,* 12(1903), 433–453. Reprinted in *Philosophical Studies* (N. Y.: Harcourt, 1922), pp. 1–30.

6. *Phil. Rev.,* 29(1920), 1–26.

7. R. A. Tsanoff, *The Problem of Immortality* (N. Y.: Macmillan, 1924).

8. G. A. Wilson, *The Self and Its World* (N. Y.: Macmillan, 1926).

9. A. C. Knudson, *op. cit.*

10. *Jour. Phil.,* 17(1920), 225–233.

11. *Proceedings of the British Academy,* 1(1903–1904), 95–98.

12. J. E. Creighton, "Two Types of Idealism," *Phil. Rev.,* 26 (1917), 514–536.

13. R. B. Perry, *op. cit.,* pp. 244, 246, 241.

14. The term "personalism," popularized in America by Bowne, has been applied to systems as diverse as those of Nietzsche and Renouvier; but it is a preferable equivalent to the older term "spiritualism," which connotes ghosts.

15. B. Bosanquet, *Logic* (Oxford: Clarendon Press, 1911), Vol. II, p. 322.

16. J. E. Boodin, *A Realistic Universe* (N. Y.: Macmillan, 1916), p. xix. In view of the statement quoted in the text, it is significant that Boodin, presiding over a section of the Sixth International Congress of Philosophy in 1926, remarked that he observed a drift toward idealism which perhaps betokened a recrudescence of idealism.

17. E. B. Holt and others, *The New Realism* (N. Y.: Macmillan, 1912).

18. J. B. Watson, *Psychology from the Standpoint of a Behaviorist* (Philadelphia: Lippincott, 1919), p. viii. See also the same author's *Behaviorism* (N. Y.: People's Institute, 1924), p. 4, etc.

19. E. B. Holt, *The Concept of Consciousness* (London: Allen, 1914), p. 114. Holt has since spoken of " what an absurd hocus-pocus " he had " conjured up " in that book, because he did not " at that time know the true locus of the ' timeless and changeless ' entities." *Jour. Phil.*, 17(1920), 377.

20. It is discussed by E. S. Brightman in the essay " Neo-Realistic Theories of Value " in E. C. Wilm (editor), *Studies in Philosophy and Theology* (N. Y.: The Abingdon Press, 1922), pp. 22–64.

21. A. N. Whitehead, *Science and the Modern World* (N. Y.: Macmillan, 1925); *Religion in the Making* (N. Y.: Macmillan, 1926).

22. B. Bosanquet, *op. cit.*, Vol. II, p. 271.

23. W. G. Everett, *Moral Values* (N. Y.: Holt, 1918).

24. J. Royce, *Lectures on Modern Idealism* (N. H.: Yale University Press, 1919), pp. 237–238.

CHAPTER VII

1. See Chapter VI of this book.

2. Such an impression is given by John Dewey, *Reconstruction in Philosophy* (N. Y.: Holt, 1920), and J. H. Robinson, *The Mind in the Making* (N. Y.: Harper, 1921), in spite of the undoubted historical scholarship of both men. The same tendency is present to

a less degree in some of the writings of the new realists. The contempt in which Kant and Hegel are held by certain moderns is a further illustration of the unfortunate tendency to disparage the past. "Many an empty head," says Berkeley, "is shook at Plato and Aristotle."

3. J. Royce, *op. cit.*, p. 233.

4. G. Santayana, *Winds of Doctrine* (N. Y.: Scribner, 1913), p. 21.

5. Ralph Barton Perry's *Present Philosophical Tendencies* (N. Y.: Longmans, 1912) and his *Philosophy of the Recent Past* (N. Y.: Scribner, 1926) reveal him as a sympathetic and competent student of the history of thought.

6. The work of Pringle-Pattison, W. R. Sorley, Josiah Royce, M. W. Calkins, R. F. A. Hoernlé, R. A. Tsanoff, G. C. Cell, and A. C. Knudson — to mention but a few — is evidence that the historical conscience is alive among idealists of various types.

7. Chapter I of the present book sketches the outlines of an idealistic psychology, and Chapter III is a start toward an idealistic theory of value.

8. J. B. Watson, *op. cit.*, pp. 19–20, 38, 14.

9. E. Jordan, *The Life of the Mind* (Indianapolis: Laut, 1925) is a step in this direction, but not a very successful one.

10. D. C. Macintosh, *The Problem of Knowledge* (N. Y.: Macmillan, 1915).

11. W. P. Montague, *The Ways of Knowing* (N. Y.: Macmillan, 1925).

12. Norman Kemp Smith, *A Commentary to Kant's Critique of Pure Reason* (London: Macmillan, 1918).

13. See E. S. Brightman, *An Introduction to Philosophy*, Chap. III.

14. R. B. Perry, "The Ego-centric Predicament," *Jour. Phil.*, 7(1910), 5–14.

INDEX

Abnormal psychology, 144
Absolute, 184
Action, 71
Activity of the self, 182, 209
Adams, G. P., 231
Adjustment, 29
Agnosticism, 149
Alcohol, 112, 113
Alexander, S., 178
American Mercury, 90
Analysis, 10–11, 58
Analytic method, 174
Approval, 69
Aristotle, 7, 18, 42, 130, 176, 207
Art, 37, 38
Athearn, W. S., 65
Athletics, 122
Aufgabe, 72
Authority of ideals, Chap. IV
Ayres, C. E., 55

Babbitt, George, 120
Bacon, F., 10, 201
Bagley, W. C., 228
Barnes Foundation, 108
Bauch, B., 222
Beautiful, 78
Beauty, 150
Behavior, 71
Behaviorism, 6, 35, 162, 205
Bentham, J., 233
Bergson, H., 209, 220
Berkeleian idealism, 168
Berkeley, G., 44, 46, 136, 236
Bermuda, 136
Bernard, C., 54
Biological situation, 15, 16
Biology, 162
Birkenhead, Lord, 133
Boas, G., 221, 223

Bolshevism, 148
Boodin, J. E., 174, 178
Bosanquet, B., 150, 163, 171, 179, 180, 181, 184, 207
Boston University, 119
Bowne, B. P., 32, 46, 127, 161, 170, 180, 181, 184, 200, 235
Bradley, F. H., 207
Brentano, F., 229–230
Bridgman, P. W., 43, 52, 54, 59, 116, 117
Brightman, E. S., 223, 230, 231, 236, 237
Broad, C. D., 37, 137
Browning, R., 101
Buddha, 130
Burns, C. D., 75
Burtt, E. A., 48
Bush, W. T., 188

Calkins, M. W., 32, 184
Canby, H. S., 107
Cassirer, E., 45, 78
Cavalier, 118
Cell, G. C., 273
Character, 65, 76
Christ, 144
Cockerell, T. D. A., 107
Coe, G. A., 29
Cohen, M. R., 108
College, 109–111, 122
Color-blindness, 17
Comte, A., 46
Confucius, 130
Constitution, national, 111
Control, 71
Courage, 97
Creighton, J. E., 165, 169, 180, 181, 189
Critical realism, 16